CHINUA ACHEBE

Nahem Yousaf

Northcote House
in association with the
British Council

For Sharon

© Copyright 2003 by Nahem Yousaf

First published in 2003 by Northcote House Publishers Ltd, Horndon, Tavistock, Devon, PL19 9NQ, United Kingdom.
Tel: +44 (01822) 810066. Fax: +44 (01822) 810034.

British Library Cataloguing-in-Publication Data
A catalogue record for this book is available from the British Library

ISBN 0-7463-1121-4 hardback
ISBN 0-7463-0885-X paperback

Typeset by TW Typesetting, Plymouth, Devon
Printed and bound in the United Kingdom by Athenaeum Press Ltd., Gateshead

Contents

Acknowledgements

I should like to thank Brian Hulme at Northcote, my family for never failing to ask how the writing of this book was progressing, and Dennis Brown and Graham Pechey for their friendship over the years.

Biographical Outline

1930	Chinua Achebe born 16 November in Eastern Nigeria, christened Albert Chinualumogu.
1948–53	Enters University College of Ibadan as an undergraduate, reading Medicine before switching to Literature. Changes his name to Chinua Achebe.
1953	Graduates from the University College, Ibadan, and begins working as a journalist for the Nigerian Broadcasting Corporation.
1958	Achebe's most well known novel, *Things Fall Apart*, is published by Heinemann.
1959	Wins the Margaret Wrong Memorial Prize.
1960	Nigeria becomes independent on 1 October. *No Longer at Ease* published. Achebe becomes the recipient of a Rockefeller Fellowship which allows him to tour Africa for six months.
1961	Marries Christie Chinwe Okoli.
1962	Becomes founding editor of the African Writers Series for Heinemann Publishers.
1964	Publishes *Arrow of God* which receives the Jock Campbell *New Statesman* Award.
1966	*A Man of the People* is published by Heinemann.
1967	Civil war. Biafra secedes from Nigeria. Achebe acts as a spokesman and fundraiser for Biafra.
1970	Civil war ends.
1971	Founding editor of the leading Nigerian journal *Okike: An African Journal of New Writing*.
1972	*Beware Soul Brother and Other Poems* wins the Commonwealth Poetry Prize. *Girls at War and Other Stories* is published by Heinemann.

1975	*Morning Yet on Creation Day* published. Achebe publishes the famous 'An Image of Africa' in which he criticizes Joseph Conrad's *Heart of Darkness*.
1976	Achebe becomes Professor of Literature at the University of Nigeria, Nsukka.
1984	*The Trouble with Nigeria*. Elected Deputy National President of the People's Redemption Party. Founder of *Uwa ndi Igbo*, a bilingual journal of Igbo studies.
1987	*Anthills of the Savannah* shortlisted for the Booker Prize. The Booker Prize is awarded to Penelope Lively for *Moon Tiger*.
1987–8	Holds the position of Visiting Fellow at the University of Massachusetts, Amherst, USA.
1988	A selection of Achebe's essays from between 1965 and 1987 are published by Heinemann as *Hopes and Impediments*.
1989	Appointed to the jury to decide the Indira Gandhi Prize for Peace, Disarmament and Development. Nominated for the presidency of PEN International.
1990	*Arrow of God* adapted as a play (*When the Arrow Rebounds*) by Emeka Nwabueze. January 1990, delivers the South Bank lecture for London Television entitled 'African Literature as Restoration of Celebration'. Spends six months in hospital following a car accident in Lagos, Nigeria, which leaves him paralysed from the waist down. Achebe receives a Triple Eminence award from the Association of Nigerian Authors.
1991	Becomes Charles P. Stevenson, Jr. Professor of Languages and Literature at Bard College.
1993	Awarded the Langston Hughes Medallion at a festival sponsored by the Schomburg Center, New York. Everyman's Library series of 'world classics' founded in 1906 adds *Things Fall Apart* to its list of titles.
1998	Achebe delivers the McMillan-Stewart Lectures at Harvard University.

1999   Appointed Goodwill Ambassador for the United Nations Population Fund (UNFPA).

2000   *Home and Exile* (Achebe's reworking of his McMillan-Stewart Lectures) published by Oxford University Press. Kwame Anthony Appiah praises the author and his work with the following: 'In all Achebe's writing there is an intense moral energy, as there is wherever he speaks about the task of the writer ... in language that captures the sense of threat and loss that must have faced many Africans as empire invaded and disrupted their lives ... his convictions are as clear and as strong and as elegantly expressed and his moral commitments as passionate as one could hope for'.

Bard College holds a weekend-long conference in celebration of Achebe's 70th birthday.

Chinua Achebe holds honorary doctorates from around forty universities and colleges.

Note: This information comes from a number of sources, including C. L. Innes, *Chinua Achebe* (Cambridge: Cambridge University Press, 1990) and Ezenwa-Ohaeto, *Chinua Achebe: A Biography* (Oxford: James Currey, 1997).

Abbreviations and References

AG   *Arrow of God* (1964, rev. 1974; London: Heinemann, 1986)

AS   *Anthills of the Savannah* (1987; London: Picador, 1988)

GW   *Girls at War and Other Stories* (London: Heinemann, 1972)

HE   *Home and Exile* (Oxford: Oxford University Press, 2000)

HI   *Hopes and Impediments* (London: Heinemann, 1988)

MP   *A Man of the People* (1966; London: Heinemann, 1988)

MYCD *Morning Yet on Creation Day* (London: Heinemann, 1975)

NLE   *No Longer at Ease* (1960; London: Heinemann, 1978)

TFA   *Things Fall Apart* (1958; London: Heinemann, 1976)

TN   *The Trouble with Nigeria* (London: Heinemann, 1984)

1

Introduction: Writing for Recovery

... the story we had to tell could not be told for us by anyone else, no matter how gifted and well-intentioned.

(Chinua Achebe, 'Named for Victoria, Queen of England', 1973)

I'm an Ibo writer, because this is my basic culture; Nigerian, African and a writer ... no, black first then a writer. Each of these identities does call for a certain kind of commitment on my part.

(Chinua Achebe, in interview with K. Anthony Appiah, *Times Literary Supplement*, 1982)

In 1993 the London *Times* declared Chinua Achebe one of 1,000 'Makers of the Twentieth Century' and in the final year of the twentieth century this progenitor of African literature and criticism turned 70 amid a flurry of accolades from around the world. Achebe is Africa's best-known novelist and *Things Fall Apart* remains the continent's best-selling novel and a world classic. Achebe began to create Nigeria's literary landscape in the years preceding Independence in 1960, but he casts back much further into the annals of precolonial history in novels that imaginatively reconstruct African and Nigerian identity in specific relation to his own Igbo ethnicity.[1] Achebe conjectures around precolonial history and myth in ways which harbour the kind of insight that is a direct result of an embattled colonial history. Despite the fact that there were other Africans publishing fiction long before Achebe began to write, he continues to be the figure most regularly represented as the originating voice in African fiction.

1

Achebe is a cultural nationalist whose fiction rests on a Fanonian belief that writing is a cornerstone of national culture.[2] Recovering the past is one component of a wider literary genealogy in which the writer begins by countering inhibiting colonial texts but invents a vast Igbo world populated with generations that span an entire century, from the 1890s to the 1980s. The world Achebe creates in his fiction is as culturally substantive as Thomas Hardy's Dorset reimagined as Wessex, William Faulkner's Mississippi reconfigured as Yokapatawha, or R. K. Narayan's Malgudi, the imaginary village in India that has sustained so many of his novels. Achebe's Umuofia is firmly situated in the Eastern Region of Nigeria. Even when his protagonists ignore their ancestral roots, or when Nigeria is recast as the imaginary African state of Kangan in *Anthills of the Savannah*, the reader is always made aware that the stories form part of an evolving mosaic.

His early work has been described as anthropological by some critics who, in their myopic concentration on the Igbo aesthetic over all other facets of his work, miss the complex web of relations – literary and cultural, national and pan-African – that form part of the *literary* process of decolonizing that Achebe undertakes with subtlety and wit. One stated goal is to prise readers away from monolithic images of empire like those promulgated and/or interpreted by two authors who continue to dominate Achebe's literary criticism to this day, Joyce Cary and Joseph Conrad, who will be discussed in detail in chapter 2. What is less frequently alluded to by Achebe, or by his critics, is the extent to which he makes his home in Eastern Nigeria representative of Nigeria as a whole, and, in turn, it is made representative of 'Africa', either by pan-Africanists or by those for whom cultural specificities need only render the writer and his work 'African'. These are issues I explore in more detail in chapter 5.

Achebe famously described *Things Fall Apart* as 'an act of atonement with my past, the ritual return of a prodigal son' (*MYCD* 70), but the speed with which national changes took place in the 1960s curtailed any easy confidence in nationhood. Almost immediately a new cloud appeared over the new independent nation, a new estrangement in neocolonial and postcolonial terms: 'In Nigeria the government was "they". It

2

had nothing to do with you or me' (*NLE* 29–30). It is to the estranged son for whom a prodigal's happy return is a tautology that Achebe turns in his second novel. In *No Longer at Ease* he takes up the topological theme of rural and urban living amidst the throes of a dying colonialism. About the neocolonial aftermath he is scathing. About Independent Nigeria he seethes. Simon Gikandi has pointed out that one critic actually intended his description of *A Man of the People* as 'a tract for the times' as a dismissal of the novel,[3] when for Gikandi, and many other readers, it is Achebe's willingness to dirty his hands in the slime of an evolving political situation that empowers his most satirical fictions with political energy. The term 'neo-colonialism' was first coined by Kwame Nkrumah, the president of Ghana, the first African country to become independent in 1957: 'The essence of neo-colonialism is that the state which is subject to it is *in theory* independent and has all the outward trappings of international sovereignty. *In reality*, its economic system and thus its political polity is directed from the outside'. The novelist Ama Ata Aidoo, formerly Minister of Education in Ghana, pursues the material consequences of shackling (black) African identities with (white) Euro-American definitions in short stories collected in *No Sweetness Here* (1974) and in the novel *Our Sister Killjoy* (1977).[4] Adewale Maja-Pearce and others have described neocolonial corruption as the dominant theme of Nigerian writing since Independence. Achebe is at the forefront with Wole Soyinka, Ben Okri – and Maja-Pearce himself in *Loyalties and Other Stories* (1986) – of literature that mounts a sustained critique of the corrupt governmental practices that have dogged Nigeria's progress since 1960.

Even when set in the past, Achebe's fictions reflect their moment of production as tellingly as the period represented. The production of historical meaning is communicated through Achebe's sense of what his benighted country needs of its writers: bold stories of cultural identity. Novels carry historical and cultural consciousness in myriad ways. Cultural critic Stuart Hall suggests that our cultural identity is never fixed or constant but 'a matter of "becoming" as well as "being" ': 'Far from being grounded in a mere "recovery" of the past, which is waiting to be found, and which when found, will serve our sense of ourselves into eternity, identities are the names we give to the different ways we are positioned by, and position ourselves within, the narratives of the past'.[5] In *Things Fall Apart* and *Arrow of God* Achebe recovers something of the dignity of precolonial ritual and custom through the telling of self-determining stories. These are stories previously untold in scribal form and peppered with proverbs that exemplify Igbo society, its family and justice systems. Each story triggers other similar stories that coalesce in a vision of Igbo civilization that may be therapeutic or cathartic for a local audience and hermeneutically stimulating for those of us who come to Achebe and to African literature from a cultural distance. Achebe is intrinsically aware that, as Franco Moretti suggests, 'the forms with which we picture historical moments to ourselves are crucial for the fashioning of our identity'.[6] In Achebe's stories history is never reduced to literalism or empiricism; what 'happens' in the past informs that same society's failures in the present, its shifting cultural values and political crises.

The Nobel Prize-winning Nigerian Wole Soyinka has described Achebe as a chronicler 'content to follow creases and stress lines, not to impose his own rearrangement on them'. Soyinka denies any disparagement is intended by the observation, pointing out that Achebe chooses to 'bring out his backcloth in relief at the areas of tension', but Soyinka has used the term chronicler pejoratively in other contexts.[7] Soyinka has always been positioned as the more unconventional and radical writer. But, within the dichotomy that this division between the acclaimed Yoruba and Igbo writers creates,[8] Achebe has been under-read. This is largely because such terms as 'chronicle' and 'saga' hold connotations of pulp or popular fiction when the national or family saga is actually an incredibly supple literary genre in which private lives can be enmeshed with public and political history in creative ways. Situating Achebe as a chronicler is easy but the ensuing danger is that he will be read as if the quality of his fiction can or should be judged according to its verisimilitude, its facility for reflecting external reality (even when that 'reality' is imagined). Achebe can be read as the paradigmatic African writer delivering a 'Nigerian' master narrative, the organizing story of a nation. Walter Ong in his classic study of orality refers to this idea as part of a culture's 'corporate retrospection', reaching back through stories to reinforce a collective cultural identity based on a shared body of knowledge.[9] This idea is inevitably anathema to poststructuralist critics of Achebe and postmodernist writers who follow his lead. However, while some socialist and Marxist African critics have usefully explored the 'sociological imagination' of African literature,[10] Flaubert, Tolstoy and Havel have seldom been charged with being 'sociological' or 'chroniclers' though they too turn the turmoil of their own nations into literature. Telling politically charged stories is dangerous for a writer in a politically volatile nation and Achebe has suffered his share of criticism as well as praise, fearing for his life on more than one occasion.

To assume that Achebe fails to problematize the nation is to fail to grasp that the past is always imaginatively reconstructed and always also philosophical. The reduction of 'Africa' to the most banal of European stereotypes demanded the excising of the continent's past, except as it could be commandeered to justify the 'savagery' of the colonized and the exigency of the imperial mission of those who come to colonize them. In *Nineteen Eighty-Four* (1948), a novel that denounces totalitarianism and capitalism, George Orwell, sickened by imperialism, imagined the place where a society's documents were taken to be destroyed as the Memory Hole. His irony turns on the recognition that the past can be obliterated if doing so serves the ends of those for whom it fails to matter.[11] Achebe succeeded in recuperating a past that had petrified into colonial representations and sunk into shame for many urban Nigerians by the end of the 1950s. He reminds his Nigerian readers of that past at the very moment that they begin to imagine their own national future after colonialization. With the publication of *Things Fall Apart* Achebe seemed to light a literary touchpaper for Nigerians and to stand quietly back; he has acknowledged that from his earliest studies of literature at university he had intended to write his own story of the nation. He imagines a subjective history for his protagonist Okonkwo while forging a collective story of Igbo precolonial days against the backdrop of what has come to be known as 'the Scramble for Africa'. European nations from Britain to Belgium coercively acquired as big and lucrative a slice of African territory as they were capable of controlling. Achebe taps into the economic and political motivation behind colonialism as well as the form it took in Nigeria. Read most positively, the story he tells encompasses a quiet warning that individual soldier-politicians, intellectuals and ethnic groups should refrain from 'scrambling' after control of the nation in a similar way. Nigeria's vast territory and cultural diversity – the Hausa-Fulani in the north, the Yoruba in the west and the Igbo in the east, as well as a very wide range of other ethnic minorities speaking a total of 200 languages – makes writing for the national recovery a difficult task.

Nigerians – those who read English – could discover something of a common index to the precolonial past in *Things Fall Apart*, before it was derided by purveyors of colonialist discourse who constructed an African history denuded of Africans and buttressed by an ideologically coherent and compelling retelling of the continent as primitive and un-civilized. Stanley Macebah of the Nigerian *Guardian* remembers the reception of Achebe's first novel in pre-Independence Nigeria: 'Achebe began to give us a picture of traditional African society that made it quite clear that our *cultures* were as respectable, as noble, as substantively important as any other culture. That did something for us' (my emphasis).[12] Ethnic rivalry between cultures would break apart the new nation and to read *Things Fall Apart* more antagonistically is to worry that in recuperating an *Igbo* past inevitably Achebe privileges and promotes a single ethnic history at a worrying period in Nigeria's history. However, from the very first he intended to create an inclusive Nigerian English: 'we can use our energies constructively in the important task of extending frontiers of the language *to cover the whole area of our Nigerian consciousness* while at the same time retaining its world-wide currency' (my emphasis). He explains, 'since I am considering the role of the writer in building a new nation I wish to concentrate on those who write for the whole nation where audience cuts across tribe or clan'.[13] But, not until *Anthills of the Savannah*, his 1987 novel, does he incorporate characters from different ethnic groups in Nigeria, as I discuss in chapter 5.

With the unparalleled success of his first novel, Achebe initiated a literary enquiry into Igbo cosmology and into nationhood that would span four more novels. In subsequent fiction, Achebe begins to formulate edgy critiques of leadership, of personal material gain at the expense of collective endeavour, and of political corruption. Rather than withdrawing to the position of chronicler after-the-fact, he engages with what is topical, in *No Longer at Ease* and, most especially, in *A Man of the People*, as explored in chapter 4. As Director of External Broadcasting for the Nigerian Broadcasting Corporation, it was within Achebe's ordinance to establish the 'The Voice of Nigeria' (also the name of the magazine in which he published a series of talks called 'Nigeria Today' in 1962). He took the commitment as a charge to 'avoid hysteria and all types of posturing' by striving to maintain a strong sense of the 'accurate' and 'objective' in topical news broadcasts.[14] He makes the case for literature quite clearly in 'What Has Literature Got to Do With It?' (1986): 'we must not see the role of literature only in terms of providing latent support for things as they are, for it does also offer the kinetic energy necessary for social transition and change' (*HI* 115).

NATION AND NARRATION

Following the international acclaim over *Things Fall Apart*, Achebe was approached to become Commissioning Editor of Heinemann's African Writers Series. He became instrumental in shaping the field of African literature as will be discussed in chapter 2. However, African literature is not a fledgling phenomenon that began with Achebe's first foray into fiction. Scholars, like Chinweizu for instance, situate twentieth-century African literature as 'a continuation (partly but only partly) in European languages, of a 5,000-year-old indigenous African tradition' that includes oral traditions rooted in African civilizations, proverbs (of which Achebe uses many), folktales, and epics.[15] As early as 1789 an Igbo published one of the first stories to detail the slave trade, *Interesting Narrative of the Life of Olaudah Equiano*. Studied often and the subject of much investigative criticism, it was lost to scholars until the 1960s when an edition was published by Paul Edwards. In 1930 black South African Sol Plaatje published *Mhudi*, a novel he had written much earlier, in 1917, in the spirit of recovery. Mhudi is a woman caught between the contrasting customs of the Matebele and the Barolong in the 1830s. The lyrical irony with which a community in transition is rendered foreshadows *Things Fall Apart*, in its recovery of an oral tradition and in its revisiting of a historical moment – the Boer Trek – from an opposing point of view. Even closer to Achebe in both time and place, novelists established as popular in Nigeria in the 1940s (Igbo Onuora Nzekwu and Yoruba T. M. Aluko, as C. L. Innes notes) were influenced by Achebe's evolving literary style, most significantly the malleability of the English language when Africanized by Achebe. Following Innes, Kofi Awoonor believes that Achebe influenced a new wave of novelists, those dealing with the cultural clash between the old and new ways in Nigerian society.[16]

Just a few years prior to the instant success of *Things Fall Apart*, Nigerian Amos Tutuola, published the glorious *The Palm-Wine Drinkard* (1952) and continued to rework the spoken Yoruba folktales with which he grew up in a series of novels and short stories. However, Tutuola's stories proved more popular on the international stage than in Nigeria where readers and reviewers were condescending in their response to Tutuola's reinvention of folktales, deeming them unworthy of serious literary consideration. Achebe remembers Nigerian students in London who averred that they hated Tutuola's first novel, and he attributes such strong feeling to their 'badly damaged sense of self' (*HE* 81). After colonialization, readers and writers from English-speaking territories were caught in something of a double bind: 'the yearning for literary expression which African writers could only satisfy at great cost of effort, will, and sacrifice, was hemmed in within the confines of a colonial system'.[17] Tutuola's work did not conform to the expectations of literature forged within colonial containment; he had spun beyond Western literary models to create what seemed to Western readers fantastical stories (Dylan Thomas was one of the few to celebrate Tutuola's breakthrough). Tutuola's writing was judged idiosyncratic so that it entered a literary cul-de-sac in African literature, as Gerald Moore famously suggested, a path that few would choose to follow until the 1980s when Ben Okri, finding the conventions of social realism too rigid, moves further beyond them than Achebe. The mythic realm of the spirit world dominates much of Okri's work, including the trilogy *The Famished Road* (1991), *Songs of Enchantment* (1993) and *Infinite Riches* (1998). Okri discloses, more than any other Nigerian writer so far, the fluid movement between the spirit and social realms on which his own and Tutuola's fictional worlds depend. Okri's fiction has proved critically popular and *The Famished Road* won him the Booker Prize while, even by his death in 1997, the pioneering storyteller Tutuola still had not received the kind of adulation Achebe enjoyed from the outset.

Achebe's distinctive popularity rests on his successful inter-penetrating of Igbo folktales and proverbs with allusions to Western literary traditions that educated audiences enjoy. Stylistically, his fusion of forms of literary realism with what he calls 'English in character', moulded to 'carry the weight of my African experience', energized African and Western readers and encouraged critics to revisit the English language to see the 'untold things' that Achebe could do with it (*MYCD* 6). Achebe has published poetry in Igbo but never fiction. It is clear that *not* writing in English has prevented some Nigerian writers from gaining more than local attention, as in the case of Hausa-Fulani writer Alhaji Sir Abubakar Tafawa Balewa whose *Shaihu Umar* (1955) was a popular bestseller in Northern Nigeria. Balewa is much more renowned as Nigeria's first prime minister murdered in the country's first coup in 1966, than as the writer of a single novel. However, *Shaihu Umar*, like *Things Fall Apart*, is set at the turn of the twentieth century and chronicles Hausa life and history in a form that is part adventure story and part travelogue. It tells a story, grounded in nineteenth-century Islamic traditions, of a good man (*shaihu*) and his trials in slavery and freedom before he finds solace in family and prayer. Reprinted many times and translated into English in 1967, *Shaihu Umar* was a popular success. While Balewa became a British knight, his government spiralled into corruption, accusing another Nigerian writer, Soyinka (whose fiercely satirical *Before the Black-Out*, 1965, denounced opportunistic politics in the new Nigeria), of taking control of a radio station in order to substitute one of Balewa's speeches to the people with another that would be self-condemning. Though finally acquitted, Soyinka was imprisoned. Achebe never makes reference to Balewa's novel.[18] A significant facet of Nigerian literary history involves the constant tension between writing and politics – and writers and politicians. Soyinka has spent many years living in exile, and self-exile and Achebe left Nigeria for the United States for four years following the civil war and continues to straddle two continents. He has made his political views known, avowing that 'what literature in Africa should be about today' is 'right and just causes' (*MYCD* 84).

Among the Nigerian writers that Achebe lists as working actively for right and just causes is Cyprian Ekwensi, a decidedly realist writer in contrast with Tutuola, who published his first novel, *People of the City*, before Achebe, in 1954. Ekwensi had actually begun his writing career by publishing Igbo folktales (*Ikola the Wrestler and Other Ibo Tales*, 1947) and popular melodrama (*When Love Whispers*, 1948) in the form of the pioneering pamphlets that came out of the market town of Onitsha in the 1940s. Onitsha is considered the birthplace of modern African writing and is situated close to Achebe's home village of Ogidi. In fact, the town appears in Achebe's fiction, sometimes named and sometimes thinly disguised, as Nkwo in 'The Sacrificial Egg' (1959), for example. Achebe was certainly aware of the literate mass audience for pulp fiction and for proletarian and white-collar protagonists like market traders and farmers, students and office workers. It is clear that such an audience buying thousands of copies of each new story could be a creative spur to writers to produce more of that genre of fiction and, for those like Achebe, to test the waters with more sophisticated interrogative fictions. In his Foreword to Emmanuel Obiechina's study of African popular literature, Achebe explains that in Onitsha education and retail trading 'sometimes got mixed up' in interesting ways.[19] In fact, Achebe taps into the Onitsha publishing phenomenon more than once in passing in his novels. In *No Longer at Ease*, Obi looks around 'the great Onitsha market' (*NLE* 42) on his way home to Umuofia after four years in England. In *A Man of the People* included on the bookshelves of an ex-teacher and now the country's Minister for Culture is *Speeches: How to Make Them*. In the same novel, on receipt of a letter from the woman he loves, the protagonist wonders how much of it may be copied from *The Complete Loveletter Writer*. Both titles are typical of the highly entertaining non-fiction Onitsha pamphlets that preached self-improvement and graced many Nigerian homes, capturing the techniques required to see oneself through the most formal of occasions or the most torrid of romantic loves.

A History of Twentieth-Century African Literatures (1993) conceives of West African writers in 'waves'.[20] It differentiates writers writing before 1964, expressing disillusion with the ways in which Independence was handled and the neocolonial backlash that undermined the nation; those writing between 1965 and 1976 focusing largely on corruption, inter-ethnic tensions and civil war; and those writing after 1976 when colonial themes give way to critiques of nation-building and the cultural crisis facing educated Nigerians, like the cast of Achebe's *Anthills of the Savannah*. Achebe writes through each of these waves. Some critics and reviewers speak of a tetralogy but others argue that Achebe's first four books mark out significant historical moments in Nigeria's national history: the 1890s in *Things Fall Apart*, the 1920s in *Arrow of God*, the 1950s and the run-up to Independence in *No Longer at Ease* and the corrupt 1960s in *A Man of the People*. A wise character in *Anthills of the Savannah*, a novel that derives intertextual resonance from the earlier fictions, declares that stories are 'the mark on the face that sets one people apart from their neighbours' (*AS* 124). In the end it is spurious to single out some novels as responding to precise historical moments since each story responds to some aspect of the Nigerian situation as it evolves. In *Girls at War* (1972), a collection of short stories written between 1952 and 1971, Achebe tackles the civil war of 1967–1970. Then, much later, once his ideas have percolated, he turns to the long-term effects of the war in his most sophisticated novel, *Anthills of the Savannah*, published in 1987.

Anthills of the Savannah, still Achebe's most recent novel, is the most self-consciously intertextual, populated as it is with wordsmiths for whom language and literature is a vocation. Earlier, in *A Man of the People* Odili, expressing his interest in a book fair devoted to the work of local authors, confides that he has ambitions to write 'a novel about the coming of the first white men to my district' (*MP* 58). Later, in *Anthills*, one character exclaims, 'I do sometimes feel like Chielo in the novel, the priestess and prophetess of the Hills and the Caves' (*AS* 114). Though unnamed, the novel to which each refers is clearly *Things Fall Apart*.

A LITERARY TESTAMENT

For the last half-century, Achebe has been involved in a reclamation process, writing for self and collective recovery after psychological and cultural dispossession and dislocation. The storyteller – or *griot* in African oral traditions – often functions as a cultural custodian and writing for recovery and legitimation is an always salient feature of Achebe's literary aesthetic. He has spoken on many occasions of the role of art in service to society and of the novelist as a teacher, but tried to eschew the studied didacticism often inherent in socially conscious literature for a more interrogative and knowing irony. Achebe's assessment of Amos Tutuola's *The Palm-Wine Drinkard* makes this clear. He argues that the novel offers 'a better, stronger and more memorable insight into the problem of excess than all the sermons and editorials we have heard and read, or will hear and read on the same subject' (*HI* 99). He has stated quite forcefully that it is the writer's duty to show that:

> African peoples did not hear of culture for the first time from Europeans; that their societies were not mindless but frequently had a philosophy of great depth and value and beauty, that they had poetry and, above all, they had dignity. It is this dignity that many African people all but lost during the colonial period and it is this that they must now regain. The worst thing that can happen to any people is the loss of their dignity and self-respect. The writer's duty is to help them regain it by showing them in human terms what happened to them, what they lost.[21]

What Achebe reconstructs in the imaginary world of the novel is a strong sense of coterminous national history in which Nigerians have a version of their past represented and verified. The facts are less important than their effects on the readership. Even in his seminal *The Historical Novel* (1962) Georg Lukacs did not specify facts as indubitably necessary to convey a sense of history, but rather as a feature of realist fiction; the underpinning of events and incidents fortifies the literary text's claims for authenticity at the level of detail. The texture of 'the past' that Achebe (re)creates in *Things Fall Apart* and *Arrow of God* was vital for a country trying to come to terms with its future on the eve of Independence when its immediate past in the throes of colonial domination was culturally debilitating. Depicting a precolonial social fabric that had a strong sense of civic polity and which was culturally complex allowed Achebe's readers to vault back over the period of colonization to take pride in traditions, even those which had not withstood the onslaught of colonialism. For example, Ezeulu in *Arrow of God* has the vital task of selecting a son to inherit his position as Chief Priest of the six villages of Umuaro. Without a moment's hesitation, Ezeulu scorns the trappings of Lord Lugard's system of 'indirect rule' when approached by a British official to become their puppet leader, as I explore in chapter 3. The voice of this tired and elderly man rings out clear in the moment that he chooses tradition over other alternatives, whatever the repercussions.

Postcolonial critics have deconstructed colonialist precepts that homogenize and flatten out notions of ethnic difference and essentialize such concepts as 'the African personality' when, as Mariama Bâ has asserted, 'Africa is diverse, divided': 'The same country can change its character and outlook several times over, from north to south or from east to west.'[22] Achebe's fiction may usefully be read in relation to developments in postcolonial studies, as Simon Gikandi does in *Reading Chinua Achebe* (1991). A conceptualization of a precolonial past is a possible starting point from which to begin to negotiate an often ambivalent and always complex African postcolonial identity, as Achebe does to best effect in *The Anthills of the Savannah*. Through an examination of Achebe's views on language, politics and power, this study will also examine the extent of his concern to represent the hybridity of post-Independence Nigeria. Achebe clearly considers himself a political writer and community spokesman, or interlocutor, for a benighted culture. In *A Man of the People* and *Anthills of the Savannah* he stays very close to government cliques, infusing his critique of post-Independence leadership with meaning for those citizens living at the mercy of military dictators who suppress the truth and order the executions of those who dare to challenge their stranglehold on the nation.

However, Achebe's fiction is much more than its political content. Achebe has spent too much time over the years explicating his preoccupation with form and style, in essays like

'Africa and Her Writers' (1963), 'Thoughts on the African Novel' (1973), 'The Truth of Fiction' (1978) and 'What Has Literature Got to Do With It?' (1986), for any study to reduce the writer simply to his context. The fiction's endurance over half a century is proof that it is much more than a cultural by-product of the struggle against colonialism, or a component of Nigeria's nation-building. It is important to recognize Achebe's artistry rather than confine him to a sub-category of sociological fiction. To take one example of textuality, at the end of *Things Fall Apart* a clansman notes that 'we must bale this water now that it is only ankle deep' (*TFA* 179). In *Arrow of God* the community is beginning to drown, but those with faith in the old ways cling to the very same natural language. Ezeulu has a nightmare in which his grandfather is standing in for him trying to address the elders of Umuaro but they shout him down: 'The Chief Priest raised his voice and pleaded with them to listen but they refused saying that they must bale the water while it was still ankle deep. . . . Then the people sensed the Chief Priest had changed from Ezeulu's grandfather to himself and began to push him from one group to another. Some spat on his face and called him the priest of a dead god'. When he wakes he feels as though he has 'fallen from a great height' (*AG* 159).

Achebe's characters are tormented by the sacking of their culture and the despoiling of their individual dignity. Different narrative strategies are employed to convey the ensuing ontological quandary: Ezeulu's disorienting and anxious fears are manifested in dreams; Obi clings to the European literary imagination, though the oblique, poetically allusive (and pathetically elusive) images he chooses fail to illuminate Nigeria. Achebe tells Obi's story retrospectively in *No Longer at Ease*, framed as it is by the legal trial at which he stands accused of bribery and corruption. Whereas Odili's unreliable first-person narrative in *A Man of the People* serves to reinforce the comedy that characterizes Achebe's most satirical novel, the interiority, Gikandi succinctly argues, shows 'how postcolonial subjects are caught up in a great ironic moment which also calls attention to their historical belatedness'.[23] The polyvocality of witness-protagonists in *Anthills of the Savannah* and its open-endedness denote a new hybridity in Achebe's literary aesthetic. A novel largely set in a literary and intellectual milieu, it is metafictional in its concern with narrative form. Out of its narrative fragments, Achebe regenerates a path back to traditional stories while projecting forward, searching for a fictional solution whereby current political atrocities and tragedies may be mediated. Achebe's oeuvre stands as a literary testament to his nation's changing historical fortunes, as in the aphorism Achebe famously contrived, 'People create stories create people; or rather stories create people create stories' (*HI* 112).

Achebe's stimulating and contentious essays elucidate his stories and are studied for their keen apprehension of the developing African literary tradition. *Morning Yet on Creation Day, The Trouble with Nigeria, Hopes and Impediments* and, more recently, *Home and Exile* deserve a book in themselves. Achebe continues to provide incisive commentary on Nigeria and on colonial and postcolonial literature while moving closer to memoir, as I discuss in my final chapter. Achebe is eclectic: as well as novels and essays, he has written stories for children, poetry (in Igbo and English) and co-edited collections of African fiction. This study concentrates primarily on the author's novels and his related criticism. Following Mikhail Bakhtin, it accepts the novel's particular alliance with modernity in reflecting 'the tendencies of a new world still in the making; it is after all, the only genre born of this new world and in total affinity with it'. Although the novel is Western in form and critics continue to debate its place in African literary traditions, Bakhtin is also helpful in asserting that the roots of the novel form should be sought in a culture's folklore. The novel nurtures and communicates what is at the core of a community's concerns and wellbeing.[24] Achebe's fiction and literary criticism comprise an important literary archive for Nigeria-in-the-making.

My rationale for the order in which the novels are discussed in this study privileges core concerns, period and setting over the sequence in which they were published. Achebe's first and third novels, *Things Fall Apart* and *Arrow of God* are examined together for their textured depiction of a traditional past. His second, *No Longer at Ease*, is discussed alongside *A Man of the People* for their incisive and bitingly satirical critique of Nigerian society in the 1950s and 1960s. *Anthills of the Savannah*

15

is considered separately, not least because it represents Achebe's return to novel writing after a gap of some twenty years. Attendant discussions of Achebe's literary responses to colonial texts and contexts, the evolving Nigerian literary tradition, and gender and representation draw on each of the novels and on short stories, as necessary. Of course, separation of the novels in this way could risk losing the line of the novelist's creative trajectory or an organic sense of an evolving fictional voice, but Achebe himself eschews chronology. He reworks the past in order to derive faith for the future. His second novel, *No Longer at Ease*, is a sequel to *Things Fall Apart* only insofar as he returns to the ur-text to pursue the genealogy of Okonkwo and his son Nwoye, continuing the discussion of father–son relationships that opened with Unoka and Okonkwo. But Nwoye's life is passed over and only conveyed in the shadow of his son's. As Gareth Griffiths suggests in 'Chinua Achebe: When Did You Last See Your Father?', Achebe skips a generation of transitional figures like his own father who 'straggle the period of cultural onslaught and change'.[25] Focusing on Obi Okonkwo's life in Lagos following his studies in England allows Achebe to probe a city on the cusp of administrative change from colonial rule to nationalist and ethnic agendas. In exploring what was a seismic shift in Nigerian politics with the onset of self-rule, there is a distinct change of tone and style. The wry and sardonic *No Longer at Ease* is a very different novel from *Things Fall Apart*; it is bitter with disappointment like *A Man of the People*. In *Things Fall Apart* the tragedy of a community breaking apart is tinged with irony but not heavily loaded with satire. Similarly, when *Arrow of God* vaults back to rural Eastern Nigeria in the 1930s, it inevitably loses the sharpness that characterizes *No Longer at Ease* in favour of a quieter evocation of a doomed generation. Whichever way one cuts the cards, Achebe writes through not one but a series of tremors in Nigeria's history: from precolonial tribal tensions to the deep trauma of colonial rule, and from colonial control to postcolonial disenchantment.

2

The Trouble with Europe: Writing Back

All Europe contributed to the making of Kurtz.

(Joseph Conrad, *Heart of Darkness*, 1902)

What [Joyce Cary's] *Mister Johnson* did for me ... was to call into question my childhood assumption of the innocence of stories.

(Chinua Achebe, *Home and Exile*, 2000)

Each man is most fully present in his own best literary work, and the Conrad of *Heart of Darkness* is the brother of the Achebe of *Things Fall Apart*.

(Cedric Watts, ' "A Bloody Racist": Achebe's View of Conrad', 1983)

There is an Igbo proverb that rings true for Achebe; it tells us that until lions produce their own historian, the story of the hunt glorifies only the hunter. When Achebe began his writing career, he set out to challenge the insidious stories in which the colonized and dispossessed are rendered inhuman and inept in order to make heroes of the 'hunter' colonialists, and to shore up the memoirs of colonial apologists. Wole Soyinka, who described him as a chronicler, as discussed in chapter 1, also refers to him as a 'crusader against the literary inequities of other writers'.[1] The comment seems double-edged but Achebe himself, remembering the tale of the lions and the hunter to exemplify what he calls the 'balance of stories' (*HE* 74), would acknowledge that he has fought long and hard against the inequities of one set of writers – empire writers – and the literary impasse into which their representations of Africa and Africans atrophied.

Colonialist ideology codified the black races as degenerate and devoid of intellectual capacity. This was a strategic ideological control that allowed colonialists to strip the colonized country of its valuable resources. Colonial texts, or empire writing, functioned cooperatively to represent 'the' African as empirical rather than cerebral and the region as a prelapsarian 'dark continent'. Empire writing was a salient component in the systematized regulation of colonial subjects, and in the recruitment of colonial adminstrators. In fact, in *Black Skins, White Masks* (1952), Frantz Fanon describes the experience of a child's first encounter with white colonial heroes and evil black savages in fiction as a primal moment. In precisely this way, Achebe recalls Joyce Cary's *Mister Johnson* (1939) and the loss of childhood innocence he describes in the epigraph to this chapter. Rather than taking place in a generic 'African' country, Cary's novel is set in Achebe's Nigeria and he does not recognize it. Achebe seeks to redress such representations that he believes pertain to his own self-image as an African and to his intention as a postcolonial writer to 'write back' to the colonial centre. He seeks to redress the imbalance he perceives in pejorative representations, and in the novels *Things Fall Apart* and *Arrow of God* he presents Africans not as stereotypes of white Eurocentric expectations who participate in cannibalism and are unable to articulate their own desires, but as sentient human beings.

The ideologies of imperialism that Achebe rejects have a long literary tradition. Characters who make their fortunes in 'the colonies' include Victorian capitalists in Jane Austen's *Mansfield Park* (1814) and Charles Dickens's *Dombey and Son* (1847) and, later, intrepid heroes who could almost be based on Henry Morgan Stanley and his travels as recounted in *In Darkest Africa* (1890). Empire adventurers are best represented in those texts which utilize the literary form of the romance or the 'boy's own' adventure story as the structuring framework for male penetrations into Africa's interior, like the novels of H. Rider Haggard and John Buchan.[2] Africa is fetishized, if not invested with desire and eroticism; in *She* (1887), and in Joseph Conrad's *Heart of Darkness* (1902) a demonic, sensual African woman can overwhelm a sophisticated European like Kurtz. Holly and Leo in Haggard's *She*, Marlow and Kurtz in *Heart of*

Darkness, and David Crawfurd in Buchan's *Prester John* (1910) all journey with a similar set of imperialist preconceptions to an 'Other' world that is the African continent. The journey is always a physical journey – the novels pseudo-travelogues – but also a psychological, exploratory journey towards the heart, or *Kor* in Haggard's case, of the imperial venture and the human condition (Sigmund Freud even refers to Haggard's *She* in *The Interpretation of Dreams,* 1900, as the heart of the unconscious).

In *She* we find the possible germination of one of *the* primary sources for Achebe's literary criticism, *Heart of Darkness*: 'Right through the heart of the darkness that flaming sword was stabbed'.[3] But, whereas *She* brings the British into an encounter with Africa's unspecific 'empire of the imagination', *Heart of Darkness* is much more specific for having an Englishman, Marlow, envoy for King Leopold of Belgium, entering the Congo. Haggard's Africa has no stated connection with empire save as a playground for European adventurers; nothing so vulgar or historically specific as imperial 'trade' is referenced. European writers at the turn of the twentieth century were mounting anthropological explorations of *Africana,* deliberately and purposefully seeking *not* to reproduce an African reality that acknowledged African history and European colonialism. Boys' magazines like *The Captain,* in which novels like Buchan's were serialized, and the *Boy's Own Paper* provided a context for the 'heroism' of colonial administrators, largely drawn from the middle classes, like the boys who read about them.[4] Black characters were often sketchily drawn; they form part of the conceptual framework of the imperial romance in which the young British hero is full of initiative and brazen confidence and the 'savage' he pits himself against must prove worthy of the test, as in *Prester John.*

Typically, however, the empire writer commodifies Africans and in so doing elides their individuality. 'The' African becomes a generic category and this is reinforced when African characters become interchangeable. Whenever they are depicted, similar language and contexts apply, as Abdul Jan-Mohamed explains:

> Just as imperialists 'administer' the resources of the conquered country so colonialist discourse 'commodifies' the native subject

into a stereotyped object and uses him as a 'resource' for colonialist fiction ... (... they all look alike, act alike and so on). Once reduced to his exchange-value in the colonialist signifying system, he is fed into the manichean allegory, which functions as the currency, the medium of exchange, for the entire colonialist discursive system.[5]

The sensibility, humanity and heterogeneity of Africans is lost to background in passages like the following from Conrad's *Heart of Darkness*: 'They shouted, sang; their bodies streamed with perspiration; they had faces like grotesque masks – these chaps; but they had bone, muscle, a wild vitality, an intense energy of movement that was as natural and true as the surf along their coast'.[6] In 'Colonialist Criticism' Achebe explains in cogent terms that 'universalism' and the universal appeal of literature is automatically ascribed to the Western writer: 'It is only others who must strive to achieve it. As though universality were some distant bend in the road you must take if you travel far enough in the direction of America or Europe' (*MYCD* 9). Even writing that describes empire as 'robbery with violence, aggravated murder on a great scale', as Conrad's does, can operate as if race *performs* culture, and Africans exist outside of culture and, consequently, outside of Western precepts of universalism.[7]

REPUDIATING CONRAD

In a lecture he delivered in 1974, 'An Image of Africa: Racism in Conrad's *Heart of Darkness*', Achebe declared Conrad 'a thoroughgoing racist' and sparked off a heated debate among critics that serves to exemplify his key role as an essayist and literary critic in what was to become a new field of critical enquiry: postcolonial studies. Achebe points to the ways in which canonical evaluation of Conrad's literary talent has masked other aspects of this modernist writer's oeuvre, most specifically Conrad's 'assault' on Africans with whom only 'distant kinship' can be claimed:

Africa as a metaphysical battlefield devoid of all recognizable humanity, into which the wandering European enters at his peril. Can nobody see the preposterous and perverse arrogance in thus reducing Africa to the role of props for the break-up of one petty European mind? The real question is the dehumanization of Africa and Africans ... And the question is whether a novel which celebrates this dehumanization, which depersonalizes a portion of the human race, can be called a great work of art. My answer is: No, it cannot. I do not doubt Conrad's great talents. . . . But all that has been more than fully addressed in the last fifty years. His obvious racism has, however, not been addressed.   (*HI* 8–9)

Achebe's comments caused a critical uproar. Cedric Watts was one of the most measured of critics who mounted a systematic rebuttal, asserting that Conrad's tale probes the very issues that Achebe says its writer endorses. Watts counters that doctrinal 'spleen' has clouded Achebe's judgement. Looking back at Watts's defence after twenty years, it loses some of its edge by a lame opening: Watts feels the need to armour himself in dissent with immediate reference to a black writer and critic who supports his view, South African Lewis Nkosi, and he assures the reader that among the images of writers and artists that surround him as he writes, Dizzy Gillespie finds place next to Shakespeare and close to D. H. Lawrence. However, both Achebe's and Watts's essays should be reread as products of their own critical moments in the history of colonial and postcolonial criticism. While Achebe deploys fighting talk in the mid-1970s, a decade later Watts is curbed by calls for authenticity in criticism, that presuppose he should declare his whiteness on entering a debate around race and representation.[8]

Of the Africanist critics who lent their voices to the fray, Ngugi admires the complexities of Conrad's narrative techniques, including the ambiguity at the heart of his representations, and D. C. R. A. Goonetilleke attempts to defend Conrad with a claim for African victimhood: he 'does not go deep into their [Congolese] lives and, from the external standpoint of a visitor, presents them as victims of imperialism who remain anonymous to him'. Felix Mnthali follows Achebe in assessing that Conrad's own attack on Europe's 'scramble for Africa' is 'neutralized' by his acceptance of 'one of the cornerstones of modern imperialism, namely, racism'.[9] Achebe defied the critical consensus that read *Heart of Darkness* as a modernist novel by conferring authorial responsibility on Conrad due to

21

his autobiographical resemblance to Marlow (*HI* 7). Returning to the argument years later, it is important to note that it is less important whether Conrad was himself racist within the late-Victorian worldview but whether the text's reception changes as a result of Achebe's dispersions.

Achebe's intervention into Conrad's *Heart of Darkness* has proved a catalyst for a critical industry that rises to the challenges of an inherently ambiguous text, one that is problematic in terms of its literary form and the authorial responsibility for the racial representations it contains. Even the situation of this work within literary debates about the canon is problematized by its having been accommodated into Leavis's *The Great Tradition* (1948) as a 'grand narrative' whilst simultaneously being read as a representative of the canon of empire that arguably reads *and* runs parallel to, *and* is contradistinctive with, Leavis's selection. The genres that coexist within *Heart of Darkness*, the sea tale, the travelogue and the adventure story, are not conciliatory with Great Literature as Leavis reads it. *Heart of Darkness* exhibits intertextual awareness of Haggard's Africa 'of the imagination' (as Benita Parry points out in her revealing study of Conrad), and extends its links to the material – the economics of empire. Furthermore, as Anthony Fothergill, following Parry, has indicated, Conrad cannot fully escape implication:

> [Africa] was an imaginative space to be escaped into; or one from which bourgeois Europe could be criticised. .... Stripped of its repressive European veneer of social mores and pretense, the authentic self waited for discovery in the landscapes of Africa. Thus, the 'savage' Other could embody the freedom that Europeans desired in order to find their 'real' selves. These uses of the imagined Africa and the 'savage', though to some extent superseded by later political and cultural requirements during the period of imperial expansion, were never quite erased. They continued to play an informing part in the discourse of the Other which Conrad assimilated.[10]

In *Heart of Darkness* Africa remains the imaginative space for potential 'self-discovery' we recognize from *She*, but is contextualized in terms of what the imperial project requires of its adventurers, that they find economic resources – ivory in this case – not just their 'selves'. Conrad's text – and hence Achebe's problems with it – might, therefore, be usefully read as a parodic imitation of a romance of empire such as *She*. It relates back to novels of this type in its rehearsal of similar motifs – a voyage, a woman loyal to the adventurer, a quest – but also stands in critical relationship to *She* and to the genre of empire as a whole, interrogating its literary conventions as it investigates a bourgeois Europe as counterpoint to a 'savage' Africa.

Although empire writing made high-flown claims for messianic imperialists, heroes in a strong masculinist tradition (like the characters in the *Boy's Own Paper*), one of *Heart of Darkness*'s variations lies in its focus and possible celebration of a type that is *not* the intellectualized hero recognizable in Haggard's Holly and Leo who set out from Cambridge University to explore Africa. It is a trope that Achebe returns to with Tony Clarke, the new colonial administrator in *Arrow of God* who muses on his tutor in Morals at Cambridge and his axiomatic phrase 'the crystallization of civilization'. Clarke tries to apply it wholesale to his own role in Africa (*AG* 108). Conrad's males do not fit: Marlow is a sailor and the listeners to his tale are named only by their occupations – a director of companies, a lawyer and an accountant.[11] These occupations provocatively signal the commercial world and the absence of the intellectualized hero within that company and, consequently, within the imperial project.[12] All five men, including Marlow and the novel's primary narrator, have had connections with the maritime empire and a practical connection with material capital, demonstrated by their situation in the metropolis on the Thames. Arguably, the reader becomes privy to a dialogue with the imperial centre incarnated in a group of listeners. This text's propensity for dialogue or double-voiced speech, which incorporates differing standpoints on imperialism, is an advance in literary form from the literary techniques employed by the writers of the romances of empire. Such romances formed a sub-genre of the nineteenth-century novel form, whereas Conrad is experimenting with a complex, fractured narrative form that we have come to associate with modernist fiction.[13]

The narrative structure is layered. One narrative is enclosed within another as in *She*, but the primary unnamed narrator's voice, the first voice we 'hear', is not only ironic and subversive but a narrative voice against which Marlow's own narrative voice contends. The story – of Marlow, of Kurtz, of Africa, of imperialism, of meaning – is decentred. As a majority of literary critics have argued, the authority of Conrad's narrative is deliberately brought into question and its ambivalence is emphasized by a struggle with language so typical of modernist works. This has a crucial bearing on the literary form; *Heart of Darkness* may generically follow the adventure story formula but it exemplifies a theoretical and technical tension between representation, form and meaning. Witness Marlow's exasperated refrain that:

> it is impossible; it is impossible to convey the life-sensation of any given epoch of one's existence – that which makes its truth, its meaning – its subtle and penetrating essence. It is impossible.[14]

For Achebe, the convolutions of the text are but 'layers of insulation' or a 'cordon sanitaire' that Conrad draws between himself and his subject matter (*HI* 7). Conrad was clearly a contradictory figure who spoke out against Belgium's King Leopold for ordering the torture and mutilation of millions of Africans in the Congo, but whose equivocating text, in Achebe's view, exacerbates the very colonial enterprise he unravels. In Conrad's fiction male characters typically find themselves trapped in a world that has no meaning; they are 'hollow men', to borrow T. S. Eliot's metaphor for modernist degeneration in the 1925 poem that takes as its epigraph Conrad's famous line, 'Mistah Kurtz – he dead'. Opacity has been one of those charges consistently laid at the writer's door even by Leavis: as he enfolds Conrad into *The Great Tradition*, he notes in an aside that the writer seems 'intent on making a virtue out of not knowing what he means'. The 'adjectival insistence upon inexpressible and incomprehensible mystery' that Leavis disparages does not extend to the Africans who are dehumanized in very precise ways: 'a burst of yells, a whirl of black limbs, a mass of hands clapping, of feet stamping, of bodies swaying, of eyes rolling'.[15] On the one hand, modernist elusiveness masks a sceptical critique of the imperialist project, of hypocritical Christianity, and of empire and modernity itself. On the other hand, the 'impressionism' that Patrick

Brantlinger and others detect in *Heart of Darkness* 'derealizes' that very critique. Brantlinger follows Fredric Jameson's lead in wrestling with what appears 'schizophrenic' in Conrad's representations.[16] Conrad was indeed aware of his contemporaries. In *Heart of Darkness* he contributes to the climate of debate that raged around two books: Stanley's *In Darkest Africa*, published in 1890, the same year that Conrad undertook his Congo journey, and General William Booth's exposé *In Darkest England and the Way Out* in 1891.

When they are merely sketchily drawn figures in a landscape, Africans are exoticized objects rather than fictional subjects. With arch contempt, Achebe observes that 'Conrad's "savages" must have had other occupations besides merging into the evil forest or materializing out of it simply to plague Marlow and his dispirited band' and that Conrad disdained to consider them (*HI* 2). It is the denial of their humanity and the attendant impression that they are aphasic that most galls Achebe because Africans are rendered silent, historically dumb, within the process of colonization. Conrad allows European characters expression and articulacy but, Achebe states, it is 'clearly not part of Conrad's purpose to confer language on the "rudimentary souls" of Africa' (*HI* 13). Achebe echoes Frantz Fanon's observation in *Black Skin, White Masks* (1952) that 'what is often called the black soul is a white man's artefact'.[17]

Conrad may have sought to satirize the high-minded colonial propaganda whereby the European imperial presence is constructive and benign, rather than destructive and malign. Indeed, the traditional linguistic connotations of 'white' and its variants are dismantled to this end. Benita Parry has demonstrated how colours operate emblematically in the text, so that 'instead of denoting purity, virtue, clarity, and veracity, white and light – which can be lurid as well as tranquil – come to signify corruption, evil, confusion and lies'. She asserts that Conrad deposes Europe from 'its self-elevation as harbinger of light in a dark continent'.[18] However ideologically subversive this may seem, Conrad does not destabilize the traditional connotations of 'black' and its variants in a similar way. Behind the 'black and incomprehensible frenzy' lies a visceral fear of black bodies; breaking up the codification of En*light*enment in order to satirize the colonizer, Conrad maintains the traditional configuration of black as evil and inferior when representing Africans. In this sense, Achebe's criticism can be understood to unsettle *Heart of Darkness*'s interrogation of colonialism to the extent to which it bases itself on the same racist assumptions that facilitate colonial expansion.

Achebe resists arguments about the social situatedness of Conrad's novels and the years have not persuaded him to review and recontextualize what was a strikingly important essay when published in 1975. While almost a founding document of postcolonial studies, often anthologized and copiously quoted, it inevitably sits uncomfortably with recent poststructuralist debates about a writer's intentionality, while the deconstructive technique of detecting unguarded moments in the work where it betrays its ideology was one of the original mainstays of postcolonial criticism. One important factor that has never changed is that Achebe takes Conrad to task for his failure to imagine the voices of Africans, who remain silenced and occluded despite their centrality in the ideological project that is his critique of the imperial enterprise in *Heart of Darkness*. Conrad fails to breach the colonial framework that he so despises. When American novelist Joseph Brodsky asked Achebe in 1988 why he had charged Conrad with racism when what he detects is merely prejudice ('but then we are all of us prejudiced'), Achebe's reply is sharp if a little weary: 'Yes, I know you do not see it. That is why I am talking about it; if you saw [racism], there would be no point talking about it. I raise it because intelligent and sensitive people like you who ought to see it, do not see it'.[19] In fact, as recently as 2000, in *Home and Exile*, Achebe castigates Elspeth Huxley in a similar manner: she is 'the griot for white settlers' (*HE* 62) in books like *The Flame Trees of Thika* (1959). In the same discussion he returns to another text that has taxed him *almost* as much as *Heart of Darkness*, Joyce Cary's *Mister Johnson* (1939).

DISPLACING CARY

Achebe's barbed attack on Cary in fiction and in essay is at once a defence of precolonial African cultures and of Achebe's right to write himself and other Africans back into literary history. Joyce Cary epitomizes the 'authentic' colonial writer. He served, not always happily, as an officer of the colonial regime in Nigeria from 1913 to 1920, returning to his experiences as Assistant District Officer in the 1930s, when he published four colonial tales, the best known of which are *The African Witch* (1936) and *Mister Johnson* (1939). Cary's letters from that time speak of isolation, a deep resentment of being exploited as a bureaucratic cog in the colonial machinery of Governor Lugard's Nigeria, the linguistic ignorance of determined monolinguals like himself, and the attendant paranoia about the social distance between himself and the Africans he fails to understand or to know. Achebe studied Cary's *Mister Johnson*, and was immediately derisive about 'the greatest African novel ever written'. For Achebe, Cary could only ever be an 'alien' writing about Africans as aliens (*MYCD* 26).

Cary writes the story of a young African clerk, Johnson, and his colonial master, Assistant District Officer Rudbeck, in Fada, Nigeria. Johnson is a thief (he steals petty cash time and again); a debtor (he never sees the error of his spendthrift ways); an embezzler (he siphons money from official funds and from local clans); and, finally, a murderer (of a man he worked for but took to robbing). The colonial administration decides that he should be hanged for the murder. Rudbeck, unable to leave Johnson to the impersonal colonial justice system, and at Johnson's request, shoots him dead. The intervening story is conveyed in the present tense in order, Cary tells us in his Preface, to create an analogy between the style and the 'cast of the hero's mind', to keep the reader's footing insecure (as if 'bushed in an unmapped country') because Johnson is such a flighty, restless young man who lives only in the present and fails to acknowledge the consequences of his actions. Johnson is Cary's buffoon: he leaps and hurls himself about and plays the fool each time he is caught in one of his scams.

Cary seems to visualize Johnson out of the tradition of minstrelsy in the United States and 1930s cinematic depictions as much as European stereotypes. Johnson's self-dramatizing is the stuff of *Gone with the Wind* (1936) and his demeanour that of an obsequious Stepin Fetchit.[20] On discovering he may be taken to court to honour his debts, he responds:

'Oh, Gawd! Oh, Jesus! I done finish – I finish now – Mister Johnson done finish – Oh, Gawd, you no fit do nutting – Mister Johnson too big dam' fool – he fool chile – oh, my Gawd.' He hits himself on the forehead with his fist. 'Why you so bloody big dam' fool, you Johnson? You happy for Fada – you catch government job – you catch good pay – you catch dem pretty girl – you catch nice gentlemen frien's – you catch new shoes – you big man – now you play de bloody fool . . .'[21]

Cary satirizes imperialism's creation of a native African elite (here 'chief clerks' to act as colonial surrogates for the district administrators), the putative beneficiaries of 'civilized' bureaucratic language who then use it as Johnson does. Johnson is a caricature with incongruous dress sense and affected English mannerisms and whereas Conrad's Congolese are inarticulate cannibals ('catch im . . . eat im'), Cary's Nigerians are pidgin-speaking incompetents. Johnson is a commodification in the way of Conrad's risible 'fireman', who is an 'improved specimen' because 'to look at him was as edifying as seeing a dog in a parody of breeches and a feather hat walking on his hind legs'. Conrad has Marlow go on, 'and he had filed teeth too, the poor devil, and the wool of his pate shaved into queer patterns, and three ornamental scars on each of his cheeks'.[22]

It is in discussing Cary in relation to Conrad that Achebe invokes one of his more biting analogies: he likens colonial fiction to totalitarian regimes who 'rent a crowd', a phrase that he says refers to a despot's facility for conjuring up crowds of demonstrators wherever necessary. Achebe recognizes Cary's 'crowd' of 'dislocated, senseless' African dancers, for example, as 'rented' from Conrad's *Heart of Darkness* (*HE* 24–6). Cary has absorbed the racial clichés of empire and Achebe parodies them, as in *Arrow of God* when Mr Wright thinks about his road gang: 'he had got very much attached to this gang and knew their leaders by name now. Many of them were, of course, bone lazy and could only respond to severe handling. But once you got used to them they could be quite amusing. They were as loyal as pet dogs and their ability to improvise songs was incredible' (*AG* 75–6). Johnson follows his hero Rudbeck in his obsessive quest to build a road in rural northern Nigeria, despite the opposition of the local Emir. It is a motif Achebe reworks with consummate irony in *Arrow of God* when the colonial decision taken is to build a road between two rival villages whose citizens have no reason whatsoever to visit one another.

However, *Arrow of God* was not Achebe's initial response to Cary. He reworks Johnson's story most overtly in *No Longer at Ease* and, as C. L. Innes compellingly shows, *Things Fall Apart* too may be read as a thematic reinvoking of Cary's story that challenges what Achebe opines is a 'superficial' depiction of Africa:

> As Cary's novel opposes the spontaneous African man of feeling inspired by the romance of European civilization to the iron rule of native conservatism or of European law, so *Things Fall Apart* contrasts Okonkwo's rigidity and refusal to acknowledge feeling . . . with the intuitive knowledge and sympathy felt by Unoka and Nwoye [the protagonist's father and son], which the latter imagines to be the property of the western missionaries. Whereas in Cary's novel these opposing tendencies cluster around European and African respectively, in *Things Fall Apart* they become associated in Okonkwo's mind – and also in the reader's – with masculine and feminine principles.[23]

C. L. Innes and Abdul JanMohamed provide elucidating readings of Cary's writing as colonialist discourse. JanMohamed indirectly supports Achebe's critique of Cary when he refutes Cary's claims to realism, and those of the majority of his critics and reviewers. He argues that Cary's 'African novels' exemplify the 'racial romance' form which involves an oversimplification of character and context through archetypes and stylized landscapes. In this reading the only real heroes can be district officers like Rudbeck (or like Cary in Achebe's correlation between text and context). In order to simplify the Africans, Cary imposes a double bind from which they are powerless to escape: they are either 'savages' whose society is petrified or the 'assimilated' (like Johnson), marginalized Nigerians who suffer the ridicule of the Europeans they seek to emulate.[24] It was left to Achebe and the generation of African writers that followed Cary to open up such closed and caricatured representations.

29

A LITERATURE OF HIS OWN

The earliest African writers to garner attention on the world stage (Tutuola, Achebe, Soyinka, Ekwensi, Camara Laye and Mongo Betti) began to publish in the 1950s, responding, on the one hand, to four centuries of colonial discourse in which 'the African personality' had suffered a barrage of pernicious epithets and, on the other, to the powerful need to tell stories that characterized the different African communities in which they were raised. Nationalist politics and racial affirmation are major issues in early examples of African literature. Writing in the 1950s and early 1960s, novelists were very aware that Nigerian schools continued to promote the English literary tradition and notions of imperial history, despite ground-breaking books like those by left-wing English historian and activist Basil Davidson that became bestsellers in Europe and America. *Old Africa Rediscovered* (1959), for example, popularized African history, coinciding with the beginnings of the Civil Rights Movement in the United States. Davidson followed it with many more revisionist histories, including *Africa in History* (1966) and *The Black Man's Burden: Africa and the Curse of the Nation-State* (1992), until his textbooks finally came to be used in African schools. When Achebe began writing he too had two very different audiences in view: English-speaking readers abroad and the local Nigerian audience. In *Morning Yet on Creation Day* he notes that sales of *Things Fall Apart* in Nigeria began to outstrip those in Britain from 1959, when it became the first novel by an African to be included for study in secondary schools across most of English-speaking Africa.

Things Fall Apart was published by Heinemann. The Heinemann African Writers series was a publishing phenomenon and the service Achebe provided as its General Commissioning Editor should not be underestimated. Through Heinemann's first 100 titles, he guided the shape of African literature. From the series' beginnings in 1962 and for the next ten years, Achebe edited Flora Nwapa, the first African woman writer to be published for an international audience; discovered James Ngugi (before he renamed himself Ngugi Wa Thiong'o) and published his novels *Weep Not, Child* and *The*

River Between, along with many more key writers in what is now recognized as the modern African literary tradition.

In 1958 when Heinemann decided to publish *Things Fall Apart*, the publisher printed as few as 2,000 copies of a novel that would go on to sell millions. It was a story by an unknown Nigerian and there was little sense of how large the market might be and no precedents to fall back on. By 1986, Achebe's own novels were selling 33 per cent of the combined sales figures for Heinemann's hugely successful African and Caribbean Writers series. His first novel's beginnings were inauspicious, however: Achebe posted the single handwritten manuscript to a typing agency in London and it languished there for more than a year. It was only much later, after the manuscript had finally been typed, that, while on a journalism course at the BBC, Achebe finally got around to offering it to Heinemann. Alan Hill, founding head of Heinemann Educational Books, remembers the first reader's report on the novel: 'This is the best first novel I have read since the war'. Nothing else needed to be said. Hill was encouraged to seek further publishing opportunities in Africa and, with Van Milne's specialized help, the series began with four books by three writers: Achebe (*No Longer at Ease* had followed quickly after *Things Fall Apart*), Kenneth Kaunda, and Cyprian Ekwensi. This was the basis of what Achebe describes as Hill's 'daring sortie into African publishing' (*HE* 50).[25]

Achebe's expertise was offered without expectation of payment and his own phenomenal literary success ensured the continuation of the series in those first years. Alan Hill sums up Achebe's significance: 'His name was the magnet that brought everything in, and his critical judgement was the decisive factor in what we published'.[26] Achebe ensured the widest possible definition of African writing through the African Writers Series. Since the first Makerere 'Conference of African Writers of English Expression' in 1952 that he returns to so often in essays and lectures, Achebe has dismissed what he refers to as 'the dogma of universality' (*MYCD* 52) in favour of a heterogeneous, continually evolving African literature. The series was 'the umpire's signal for which African writers had been waiting at the starting line' (*HE* 51). His association with Heinemann may have ended with their hundredth title,

31

his own *Girls at War* (1972), but what he often refers to as the 'first generation' of modern African writers had already ensured that the 'inhibiting non-identification' that Achebe felt as a young African reader of European fiction was 'a thing of the past' (*MYCD* 40). Young Africans from the 1960s on have been granted access to a literature of their own and Achebe was instrumental in bringing that about.

Achebe began to publish his literary criticism while commissioning works for Heinemann and writing his own inimitable fiction. It would not be unjust to say that the essays are largely a form of autobiography. Recalling his university education at Ibadan in the 1940s, for example, Achebe describes being expected to study the same literary models as students in Britain. But his eyes soon opened to their ideological content:

> When I had been younger, I had read these adventure books about the good white man, you know, wandering into the jungle or into danger, and the savages were after him. And I would instinctively be on the side of the white man. You see what fiction can do; it can put you on the wrong side ... In the university I suddenly saw that these books had to be read in a different light. Reading *Heart of Darkness*, for instance, which was a very, very highly praised book and which is still highly praised, I realised that I was one of those savages jumping up and down on the beach. Once that kind of Enlightenment comes to you, you realise that someone has to write a different story. And since I was in any case inclined that way, why not me?[27]

Achebe is a novelist and literary critic whose reading and writing experience fostered African literary criticism and fostered the literary and critical work of others. In 1990 a festschrift for Achebe elicited poems from Ama Ata Aidoo, and recollections from his earliest critics and reviewers like G. D. Killam and Biodun Jeyifo. More recently, Toni Morrison has said that what she gained from reading Achebe's work was the courage not to write in response to or against 'the white gaze' but to 'postulate its irrelevance'.[28] Achebe has proved himself a transgressive critic as well as a groundbreaking writer. *Things Fall Apart* is taught alongside Joseph Conrad's *Heart of Darkness* and is as universally acclaimed (despite Achebe's impatience with the term) as any twentieth-century fiction.

Similarly, whenever an essay collection or conference addresses *Heart of Darkness*, it cannot but take account of Achebe's criticism. This study tries to convey something of the scope and depth of Achebe's work, but it is the African novel that Achebe has dominated for so many years, and the novels discussed in the chapters that follow for which he will always be best remembered.

3

The Past is Another Country: *Things Fall Apart* and *Arrow of God*

Let no one be fooled by the fact that we may write in English for we intend to do unheard of things with it.

> (Chinua Achebe, 'Colonialist Criticism', 1974, in *Morning Yet on Creation Day*, 1975)

Every community has enough firewood in its own forests for all the cooking it needs to do.

> (Chinua Achebe, 'My Home Under Imperial Fire', in *Home and Exile*, 2000)

Translated into more than fifty languages and with sales of more than eight million copies, Achebe's first novel begins the literary project that tracks Igbo history from tradition to modernity. It is generally accepted that West African countries did not undergo a deep colonization, but rather what has been (somewhat ironically) described as a 'benign colonialism' which took place through missionaries and administrators rather than the military or land speculators. This is how Lord Lugard's system of 'indirect rule' would work, using tribal leadership to effect colonial administration. But Christian missionaries, benign or otherwise, aimed to change the mind-set and the belief systems of the peoples they encountered. In line with what they called their 'civilizing mission', they sought to convert the 'natives' to Christianity, while, in the process, ridding them of their 'primitive' beliefs. Indeed, in *Things Fall Apart*, the missionaries have come to Okonkwo's village, Umuofia, 'built their church there, won a handful of converts and were already sending evangelists to the surrounding towns and villages' (*TFA* 101). Fissures appear in precolonial society with the arrival of the first Christians and the erosion of traditional values progresses steadily.

Achebe began writing his first novel in 1956, having cogitated on the story he would tell since around 1954. The publication of *Things Fall Apart* in 1958 fell on the eve of Nigeria's official independence in 1960 and yet the story harks back to the turn of the century. This is clearly of strategic importance because the novel is a concerted attempt to reconstruct – and to construct for the first time in scribal form – a dignified public past. The novel indicates how a traditional Igbo lifestyle was disrupted by the advent of colonialism, together with the Igbos' own internal processes of change and development. On the eve of Independence Achebe issues a warning that forgetting the past is an obstacle to changing the future, and alerts his readers not to allow the kinds of flaws he detects in a precolonial tribal system to mar the new nation's chances of success. One of the most salient features of Igbo culture is the lack of tolerance for individual leaders whether in the form of chiefs or kings. In fact, in such a republican community there is even a name, Ezebuilo, that means 'a king is an enemy'. In Igbo cosmology, even the supreme deity who communicates through an oracle is understood to be a communal voice. Where the Igbo form of feudal democracy fosters individualism, it does so in the form of self- and group-rule epitomized by and sanctified by the *chi*, a god-agent in the spirit world who parallels each individual on earth: 'The world in which we live has its double and counterpart in the realm of the spirits' (*MYCD* 94). The *chi* forms the basis of many cautionary tales in Igbo tradition ('when a man says yes his *chi* will also agree: but not always') and the stories of Okonkwo (and of Ezeulu in *Arrow of God*) are extrapolations from such tales. Achebe informs us that 'the Igbo are unlikely to concede to the individual an absolutism they deny even to *chi*. The obvious curtailment of a man's power to walk alone and to do as he will is provided by another potent force – the will of his community' (*MYCD* 99).

TEXTUALIZING THE PAST

The story Achebe tells in *Things Fall Apart* is primarily that of Okonkwo, a wealthy farmer, an acclaimed wrestler, a warrior and a highly respected member of the Umuofian clan. Although still young, Okonkwo is 'already one of the greatest men of his time' (*TFA* 7). He excels within the world he knows, but his failure lies in his impulsiveness and in his inability to take considered advice, even from those he trusts, on how he should conduct himself, especially when the world he knows begins to change with the onset of colonialism. When he oversteps clan rules, the elders are sensitive on many occasions and the punishments they decree are apt and fair. When Okonkwo commits a sin against the feminine principles that his society holds sacred, he is exiled to his mother's home of Mbanta. Returning after seven years he finds Umuofia changed; even dedication to Igbo ritual is tempered by the effect of the Christian church. The village structure has been weakened by the presence of the missionaries and district administrators on its edges. The Igbos are fascinated by the Christians' apparent disdain for Umuofia's most powerfully negative forces: they build their church in the middle of the Evil Forest yet no evil befalls them. Achebe demonstrates that it is the language, symbol and ritual that the Christians use that affords them a way to penetrate this traditional society and the converts they make to begin with are inevitably those who live at the margins themselves, like the *osu* or outcasts. Little by little, where others in Umuofia submit to the inevitability of change, Okonkwo cannot. The final impulsive act, when he beheads a messenger sent to the clan by colonial administrators, precipitates his tragic end. When Okonkwo's action prompts no further violence on the part of the clan against the colonialists, he knows his stature in the community cannot overcome the inroads they have made. He commits suicide.

When Achebe returns to traditional Igbo societies in the 1930s in *Arrow of God*, he tells the story of another brave man who tries to live within the powers bestowed on him by his community. But his fear of the erosion of the culture he epitomizes, personal ambition and a certain hidden power-hungry demagoguery finally persuade him to overstep his responsibility to the clan. Ezeulu, the Chief Priest and protector of the security of the six villages of Umuaro, is at the heart of a community breaking apart at a more accelerated rate than Umuofia in *Things Fall Apart*. Around the tragic stories of Okonkwo and Ezeulu, Achebe sets about textualizing Igbo cultural identity. As social critic Stuart Hall contends, literature's function in the ideological construction of cultural identity works through 'memory, fantasy, narrative and myth'. Achebe deploys each to creative effect in *Things Fall Apart*. His facility for textualizing the quotidian with symbolic resonance makes the novel a fictionalized history with the power of myth: 'There is a saying in Igbo that a man who can't tell where the rain began to beat him cannot know where he dried his body. The writer can tell people where the rain began to beat them'.[1] As Wole Soyinka points out in his assessment of *Arrow of God*, 'the gods are made an expression of the political unity (and disunity) of the people. Their history or measure (or both) testifies to their subjection to secular consciousness'.[2]

The myths Achebe discloses are also keenly politicized. One African literary critic, Chidi Amuta, lists a number of types of realistic formulas he sees operating in African fiction. Following Abdul JanMohamed, he detects critical realism in much of Achebe's work and socialist realism in novels by Kenya's Ngugi wa Thiong'o. If we accept Amuta's taxonomy of forms of realism, underpinning Achebe's critical realism is the measured voice of the narrator who acts as teller/observer and commentator/investigator. The writer takes on the role of witness and the narratorial mode is naturalistic, reproducing a detailed texture of a 'real' world in the imagined world of the novel.[3] *Things Fall Apart* and *Arrow of God* are studded with examples of ritual and tradition: initiation and betrothal rites; death rituals; festivals like the Week of Peace and the Feast of the New Yam; the worshipping of ancestral spirits, sometimes personified by tribal elders (the *egwugwu*) and usually by the *Agbala*. A network of folkways sustains the Igbo villagers and their ceremonies. The scenes Achebe describes embody this civilization's key philosophical relationships: the living with the dead, the natural with the supernatural, the past with the present, and the balance of this society's feminine principles with masculine mores.

In both *Things Fall Apart* and *Arrow of God*, Achebe seeks to produce the effect of a precolonial reality as an Igbo-centric response to a Eurocentrically constructed imperial 'reality', as discussed in chapter 2. Achebe's realism should be understood in historical and ideological terms, as he, in turn, purports to understand Conrad's in *Heart of Darkness* (Mineke Schipper refers to Achebe's criticism of that text as firmly based in a 'text-reality' paradigm[4]). *Things Fall Apart* defines itself against the District Commissioner's idea of a sociological-anthropological narrative of Africa, a text he calls *The Pacification of the Primitive Tribes of the Lower Niger* in which Okonkwo could form part of a decent paragraph. This 'text' is first mentioned in the final paragraph of *Things Fall Apart* when the Umuofians even offer to pay the colonizers to bury Okonkwo because their religious beliefs forbid them from touching the body of a man who has taken his own life. In purposeful contrast, the novel that precedes the District Commissioner's verdict defines its reality from the perspective of the colonized Nigerian. A specifically Igbo ontology and cosmology is elevated over a Eurocentric world-view. To read the novel as a correction of Eurocentric depictions of Africa is to recognize the impact of the final pages when the District Commissioner's words deny Okonkwo and the clan he tried to represent in his passionate struggle against change:

> In the many years in which he had toiled to bring civilisation to different parts of Africa he had learnt a number of things. . . . In the book which he planned to write he would stress that point . . . he thought about that book. Every day brought him some new material. The story of this man who had killed a messenger and hanged himself would make interesting reading. One could almost write a whole chapter on him. Perhaps not a whole chapter but a reasonable paragraph, at any rate. There was so much else to include, and one must be firm in cutting out details. (*TFA* 183)

His characterization of Okonkwo as material colonizes the Igbo warrior even in death. Achebe's protagonist may be commandeered merely as a swift exemplification of colonial etiquette; a district commissioner does not cut down from a tree a savage who, in his savagery, has killed himself.

In *Arrow of God* Achebe returns the reader to *Things Fall Apart* with consummate irony when the book is attributed an author, George Allen, and published. *The Pacification of the Primitive Tribes of the Lower Niger* has already become a colonial classic, a manual of empire-building circulating between colonialist characters Captain Winterbottom and Tony Clarke. Fifty years later, in the setting of *No Longer at Ease*, Okonkwo's grandson Obi idly considers writing a counter-text, the tragedy of the colonizer whose unassailable position in the grand colonial scheme is becoming vulnerable as the country lurches towards Independence: 'In 1900 Mr Green might have ranked among the great missionaries; in 1935 he would have made do . . . but in 1957 he could only curse and swear.' Green has, Obi muses, succumbed to the 'incipient dawn' of Independence rather than the 'darkness' that envelops Conrad's Kurtz (*NLE* 96–7).

Achebe has specified on countless occasions that African writers inevitably find themselves in a dialectical relationship with white Western cultures, literary traditions and representations in which the act of writing becomes a polemical 'writing back' to the metropolitan centre. In this context *Things Fall Apart* becomes counter-cultural. It disrupts the hegemony of colonial discourse, operating as it does in a dialogic relationship with colonial literatures. Achebe responds to what Abdul JanMohamed defines as the overt aims of colonialism: he explains that the colonizers' covert purpose is always to exploit natural resources 'thoroughly and ruthlessly through the various imperialist material practices', but that the overt aim is to 'civilize' the savage; 'to introduce him to all the benefits of Western cultures'. In colonial discourse, this aim is embedded in historical texts and in literature in which the 'savagery' of the colonized peoples justifies occupation and exploitation: 'If such literature can demonstrate that the barbarism of the native is irrevocable, or at least very deeply ingrained, then the European's attempt to civilize him can continue indefinitely, the exploitation of his resources can proceed without hindrance, and the European can persist in enjoying a position of moral superiority.'[5] JanMohamed terms this ideological framework 'the manichean allegory' – a series of oppositions or binaries – white versus black; positive versus negative; civilization versus savagery; self versus other; and active subject versus passive object.

39

Before postcolonial critics articulated these ideas in theoretical terms, Achebe was openly and passionately concerned that African identities had been essentialized and commodified, as discussed in chapter 2. In his earliest fiction, Achebe transgresses the boundaries of received representations, subverting the authorized version of Africa (not only the District Commissioner's text in *Things Fall Apart*, but also colonial discourse in general). For example, where empire writing conforms to a light/dark lexicon wherein stereotypes of blackness are bestial and primordial, *Things Fall Apart* defamiliarizes whiteness so that its hegemony is broken apart. Before white men arrive in Umuofia, there are stories circulating of 'white men who, they say, are white like this piece of chalk . . . And these white men, they say, have no toes'. Achebe defamiliarizes the white Western strangers through their custom of wearing shoes, just as their bicycles become 'iron horses'. In Igbo culture, leprosy is known as 'white skin' and one man makes a joke, 'one of them passes here frequently . . . His name is Amadi' (*TFA* 64–5). (The dissonance derived from such a joke is a technique on which Toni Morrison signifies to differing effect in *Beloved* in 1988, when Beloved fears the 'men with no skin'.) In *Things Fall Apart*, white men are initially an object of ridicule but the story of the village of Abame changes that. (It is a story to which Achebe has Igbos return later in *Arrow of God*.) It is a 'strange and terrible story' in which a white man appears in the clan. At first he is taken for an albino, but the Oracle of Abame has prophesied that a strange white man will be the harbinger of white 'locusts'. They kill him out of fear and in a reprisal are themselves wiped out: 'Their clan is now completely empty. Even the sacred fish in their mysterious lake have fled and the lake has turned the colour of blood. A great evil has come upon their land as the Oracle had warned' (*TFA* 120–2).

UPSETTING THE UNIVERSAL

Things Fall Apart is a groundbreaking African novel in its purposeful unsettling of whiteness. In 1958 Achebe chips away at the consensus of whiteness thirty years before the first theoretical extrapolations on white racial identity (signalling the beginning of whiteness studies with essays like Richard Dyer's iconoclastic 'White' of 1988, for example). Achebe begins to unhobble the literary imagination foreclosed by empire.[6] In *Things Fall Apart*, it is the very pervasiveness of Igbo cosmology that provides a specific account of whiteness. Christianity too is seen as absurd when viewed through the lens of the Igbo belief system, until that system is in danger of being overturned: 'The white man is very clever. He came quietly and peaceably with his religion. We were amused at his foolishness and allowed him to stay. Now he has won our brothers, and our clan no longer acts like one. He has put a knife on the things that held us together and we have fallen apart' (*TFA* 155–6).

In a simple reversal of the tradition of caricatured Africans in colonial texts, Achebe satirizes the idea that all Englishmen are alike: the names Mr Brown and Mr Smith are deliberately generic. However, after the initial wry smile, the two missionaries function more seriously as interlocutors of Christianity as colonialism. Mr Brown functions to reflect the supposedly benign colonialism that Nigeria experienced compared to other African countries. He has a certain quiet respect for those he has come to convert. He is incapable of viewing the Africans' religious beliefs as equal in worth to those he holds as true, but he takes the time to learn about Umuofian religious tenets from Akunna, a man of rank and sensibility, debating with him through an interpreter. His successor the Revd James Smith is unwilling to perceive Africans as anything other than savages. His yardstick is Caliban, the quintessential colonial subject and tellingly in Achebe's ideological context a literary construct that has colonized the Western imagination. Mr Smith combines brutal force with religious fervour. He condemns what he sees as Mr Brown's 'policy of compromise and accommodation' because, the narrator adds ironically, 'He saw things in black and white. And black was evil. He saw the world as a battlefield in which the children of light were locked in mortal conflict with the sons of darkness' (*TFA* 162). In this way the novel works as an exposé of the missionaries' myopia with regard to Africa. But the novel is more complex than a straightforwardly reversed representation; such myopia was a necessary component of the colonial discourse that supported imperialism. Achebe critiques this as he creates a society at the mercy of imperialism.

What most of the earliest reviewers did not choose to focus on was the novel's importance as a cultural and literary statement about the kinds of quotidian reality colonialism sought to undermine. *Things Fall Apart* is not 'universal', though it was carefully positioned as such by critics in order to ease its assimilation into a Western canon. Western discourse has, of course, controlled the definitions of 'universal' and 'human'. Achebe has actually advocated that the term 'universal' be debarred from discussions of African literature 'until such time as people cease to use it as a synonym for the narrow, self-serving parochialism of Europe'. He repeats this idea with specific reference to Eldred Jones's description, in *Introduction to Nigerian Writing*, of Wole Soyinka's corpus of work as 'universally valid' (*MYCD* 52). Literary criticism of this type would also seem to deny any celebration of ethnic African identities. *Mbari* is the Igbo term that Achebe uses. It conveys the indivisibility of art and society as epitomized in the 'house of images' built to celebrate artistry for the goddess *Ala*.[7] Early critics mistakenly saw the sole motive behind African literature as integration into Western literary forms, with the African writer represented as what Achebe has termed an 'unfinished European' who will, subsequent to a thoughtful apprenticeship, learn to write like Europeans (*MYCD* 3). In order to assimilate the novel into Eurocentric models, critics have had to either ignore its Igbo cosmology, designate it as quaint and fabulous rather than specific, or emphasize the novel's tragic structure within recognizably Western frameworks. For example, Achebe is quite specific about Okonkwo's failings:

> his whole life was dominated by fear, the fear of failure and weakness. It was deeper and more intimate than the fear of evil and capricious gods and of magic, the fear of the forest, and of the forces of nature, malevolent, red in tooth and claw. Okonkwo's fear was greater than these. It was not external but lay deep within himself. It was the fear of himself, lest he should be found to resemble his father. Even as a little boy he had resented his father's failure and weakness ... and so Okonkwo was ruled by one passion – to hate everything that his father Unoka had loved. One

of these things was gentleness and another was idleness. (*TFA* 12–13)

Okonkwo's fears derive from an Igbo world-view (except for his debunking of his father for which there exists no tradition in a society that 'judges a man according to his worth, and not according to the worth of his father', *TFA* 7). But, then, as if to tease, Achebe adds the phrase 'red in tooth and claw', parenthetically. Okonkwo is often read as a tragic hero in the Aristotelian and Shakespearean senses, and David Carroll has compared Okonkwo to Thomas Hardy's Michael Henchard in *The Mayor of Casterbridge*. Achebe has been written about as a direct literary disciple of W. B. Yeats and T. S. Eliot, with specific reference to *Things Fall Apart* and *No Longer at Ease* due to his appropriation of their poetry in the titles of his novels. 'Things fall apart' is, of course, a quotation from Yeats's 'The Second Coming' and 'no longer at ease' a phrase from Eliot's 'The Journey of the Magi', in which the wise men discover that after the birth of Christ they are no longer at ease with 'the old dispensation'.

The irony with which Achebe reorients Yeats's idea of history as an evolving succession of civilizations, each phased out by its inability to be truly democratic or inclusive, should not be lost, whether the civilization in question be European or African. The *osu* are a case in point. *Osu* are outcasts because they are descended from slaves to gods of the clan and are described as present in late nineteenth-century Igbo society in *Things Fall Apart*. However, they remain socially excluded in the 1950s in *No Longer at Ease*. Clara Okeke is a beautiful young woman and successful in her nursing career, but her life is circumscribed by fear and prejudice half a century later. When Obi wishes to marry an *osu* his mother curses him, 'If you do the thing while I am alive, you will have my blood on your head because I shall kill myself' (*NLE* 123). Even his father, a retired catechist who has devoted his life to his Christian beliefs laughs 'as if through a throat of metal': 'It was the kind of laughter one sometimes heard from a masked ancestral spirit' (*NLE* 120). He even uses a biblical analogy to liken Naaman the leper to the Okeke family ('do not bring the mark of shame and leprosy into your family'). Across Achebe's fictions, the 'new religion' becomes an option for those who feel themselves unrepresented within Igbo belief systems and social structures. In the story 'Chike's School Days' (1960), for example, an *osu* family's Christianity leads a young boy to refuse a neigbour's offer of food because 'We don't eat heathen food': 'The neighbour was full of rage, but she controlled herself and only muttered under her breath that even an *Osu* was full of pride nowadays, thanks to the white man . . .' (*GW* 36). What becomes clear as one situates Achebe's early work in the Nigerian context is that Achebe's primary interest lies in the myriad, and sometimes surprising, effects of colonialism on his own (representative) community.

Rather than provide an idealized picture of a precolonial African society, Achebe interrogates its flaws as well as its qualities. He critiques individual and patriarchal excesses via Okonkwo, and the society's susceptibility to economic bribes by the colonial regime. Social imbalance is the crucial danger since the society Achebe depicts rests on two sets of values that he defines as masculine and feminine. In order for Umuofian society to function harmoniously both strands have to be respected and represented. Okonkwo sublimates the factors in his upbringing that he perceives as feminine because he associates them with his father Unoka's failure, an idea to which we will return in chapter 5 where issues of gender are discussed. Okonkwo is unbalanced: he follows an individual-istic line while his society emphasizes that the community is greater than the individual. *Agbala* is a masculine god whose voice is that of the supreme goddess and whose will is mediated through a priestess, another female. When the priestess carries Okonkwo's daughter Ezinma to see *Agbala*, both Okonkwo and his second wife follow, distrusting the meaning of *Agbala*. The priestess's curse that seems to apply to Ezinma's mother is in fact anticipatory of the form that Okonkwo's own death will take: 'Somebody is walking behind me. May he (*Agbala*) twist your neck until you see your heels!' (*TFA* 92). *Agbala*, the spiritual parent of the clan and both male and female, is a reminder of the importance of balance and symmetry in the community. In denying *Agbala*, Okonkwo denies the earth goddess and, it is suggested, predetermines his suicide – an offence against the earth. Even Okonkwo's movement, his manner of walking, denies the earth; we are told that feet should be 'set flat and firm upon the earth' but when Okonkwo walks 'his heels hardly touched the ground, and he seemed to walk on springs' (*TFA* 4). The text is studded with examples, proverbs and similes that pinpoint Okonkwo's imbalance in terms of Igbo cosmology. Most significantly Okonkwo denies his *chi*, the ultimate signifier of balance in this society:

> The Igbo people . . . immediately set about balancing this extra-ordinary specialness [the *chi*], this unsurpassed individuality, by setting limits to its expression. The first limit is the democratic one that subordinates the person to the group in practical, social matters. And the other is a moral taboo on excess which sets a limit to personal ambition, surrounding it with powerful cautionary tales. (*HI* 39)

Although not referring directly to *Things Fall Apart*, this definition serves to elucidate the taboos that Okonkwo breaks on many levels and on many occasions. His life is a cautionary tale. Okonkwo dies not only because he challenges the colonizer but – and significantly from an Afrocentric view – he dies because he sets himself above his *chi* and refuses to be reconciled to the feminine principle in Igbo belief even after seven years in his maternal homeland. Okonkwo contributes to his own downfall; he is not a victim of colonialism alone.

Okonkwo is not an uncomplicated metaphor for his society and its demise: he commits a series of crimes against it. Achebe cannily deploys Okonkwo to assert the need for balance in contemporary Nigerian society at the end of the 1950s if it is to reassert a collective African identity through which to withstand the hazards of Independence. Balance is a key preoccupation of Achebe's in *Things Fall Apart*. Having described himself on the personally political level as living at the crossroads of two cultures, Achebe cast off his English christened name of Albert just prior to the novel's publication. *Things Fall Apart* is 'an act of atonement with my past, the ritual return and homage of a prodigal son' (*HI* 25) as if his character Nwoye had come to re-evaluate the society he leaves behind in the novel.

WHEN TWO WORLDS COLLIDE

Achebe is often referred to as a 'man of two worlds', a writer 'in transition' or 'at the crossroads'.[8] These are organic metaphors which aim to convey something of his facility for portraying past struggles to maintain pride in a precolonial cultural identity and contemporary struggles in the crucible of modernity – and the ongoing tension between the two worlds. Achebe operates out of a series of dialectical tensions across the novels ('Wherever Something stands, Something Else will stand beside it. Nothing is Absolute', *MYCD* 94). However, Achebe is neither ambiguous nor ambivalent in his claims to *straddle* two 'worlds'. He often refers to the conjunction as 'two streams meeting' and the tension that inevitably results as useful for an artist. For example, he describes learning about Christianity from his parents and Igbo traditions from his larger social environment, allowing that Igbo folktales caught his imagination far more readily than biblical parables. So he offers his readers the idea of the crossroads as a creative space or 'zone of power' in which stories are made. This idea is exemplified in Achebe's third novel set in the six villages of Umuaro, *Arrow of God*. The villages have forged a community and have even imagined into being a deity, Ulu, the invention of a tradition that serves to bring into studied alignment the disparate, even antagonistic, villages and their representatives. The story revolves around Ulu and his representative, half-man, half-spirit Ezeulu, who is symbolically split between his ritualistic role (one half of his body is painted white for each ceremony he conducts) and his role as Igbo male – husband, father and elder. In this novel Achebe also comments meaningfully on the fashioning of 'traditions' by the Igbo and by colonial administrations.

Tony Clarke is a newly minted colonial appointment, two weeks into his first stint as deputy to Captain Winterbottom. He muses grandly on what he sees as his new role, to protect 'his natives' from the acts of 'thoughtless white people' – other than himself, of course (*AG* 162). When greatness is foisted upon him in the absence of Winterbottom a very few pages later, standing in for his superior he insults Ezeulu by offering him a fabricated colonial 'title' that deprecates his Igbo heritage and cultural standing:

'Well are you accepting the offer or not?' Clarke glowed with the I-know-this-will-knock-you-over-feeling of a benefactor.

'Tell the white man that Ezeulu will not be anybody's chief except Ulu.'

'What!' shouted Clarke. 'Is the fellow mad?'

'I tink so sah,' said the interpreter.

'In that case he goes back to prison.' Clarke was now really angry. What cheek! A witch-doctor making a fool of the British Administration in public! (*AG* 174–5)

It is the Department of Native Affairs' decision to appoint Warrant Chiefs as a mechanism in the establishment of 'indirect rule', a decision with which the seasoned colonialist Winterbottom disagrees. The decision to call Ezeulu to head office and to imprison him for an unspecified period when he refuses the 'honour' of the fabricated title lies behind the delay of the Festival of the New Yam: a traditional festival on which a people depends is jeopardized. The yams that should feed the six villages are ruined because Ezeulu is unable to perform the ceremony that marks the agricultural calendar. The yams rot in the earth and Ezeulu becomes the arrow (or messenger) of a god (Ulu) who pierces the heart of the Umuaro community, forcing it to its knees by clinging to his ritual role in the face of real physical hardship. The dramatic centre of *Arrow of God* and its unifying figure, Ezeulu is ironically as much the cause of his society's weakened state as his hot-headed precursor Okonkwo. Initially the shrewd compromiser, Ezeulu becomes intransigent when he refuses to eat the three remaining seed yams as a prelude to the harvesting of the new crop. He becomes a literalist who cannot sanction the festival without seeing a new moon for each yam he eats. The crisis returns the reader to the opening pages of the novel when his age-old fear of the new moon is overcome only by the pride he feels in his office.

Ezeulu is reluctant to rely on anyone's judgement but his own: he 'did not like to think that his sight was no longer as good as it used to be and that some day he would have to rely on someone else's eyes'. The physical stands in for the moral strength that Ezeulu sometimes lacks: 'for the present he was as good as any young man or better because young men were no longer what they used to be. ... Whenever they shook hands with him he tensed his arm and put all his power into the grip, and being unprepared for it they winced and recoiled in pain' (*AG* 1). When his favourite son dies, his strength is weakened. Obika's death may have been natural after a long and arduous run, but he is weakened by malnutrition and it cleaves the old man's mind in two (the 'two worlds' that Achebe has chronicled and critiqued cannot be reconciled) and he can borrow strength from no one. Obika is the most handsome of men (*Ugonachumma*) and, much like Okonkwo, he is fearless, a firebrand: he ousts a wicked medicine man from his compound in a single athletic move, to the joy of a watching crowd (*AG* 198). It is emphasized that 'a man like him did not come along too often' (*AG* 228). The old man's final days are spent in grief, in the 'haughty splendour of a demented high priest' that frees him from the consequences of his calamitous decision (*AG* 229). As with Okonkwo, Obika's physical death signals the loss of the old dispensation: 'what could it point to but the collapse and ruin of all things' (*AG* 229). Although Ezeulu describes himself as his community's 'watchman', by the end of the novel he has been tempted to abuse the power borrowed from Ulu, the deity whose representative he is. Like Okonkwo, Ezeulu has forsaken his individual responsibility to the group and the group's beliefs. He breaks tradition partly in the sin of pride in his own ability to judge a case, as when he counsels Umuaro against war with Okperi and supports Captain Winterbottom. He invests Captain Winterbottom with symbolic significance as the 'Destroyer of Guns' and prides himself that they have a special relationship, even though to Winterbottom he is merely 'that impressive-looking fetish priest' (*AG* 59). In so doing he underestimates the long-term effects of internal divisions like the central battle for Umuaro's support waged by Nwaka and the priest of Idemili against Ezeulu.

In *Arrow of God* Achebe chooses a narrative structure that alternates the story of traditional village life in the 1920s with chapters in which the colonial administration is firmly established. One character muses sadly: 'I have travelled in Olu and I have travelled in Igbo and I can tell you that there is no escape from the white man. He has come'. The speaker cites the lost village of Abame and adjudges, 'As daylight chases away darkness so will the white man drive away all our customs' (*AG* 84). In this novel, although Government Hill houses only five officials, they are deeply ensconced in the material life of Nigeria: building roads and sewers, like Rudbeck in *Mister Johnson*. Achebe refers back to a programme of road building three years prior to the action of the novel, during which a notorious overseer intimidated villagers and levied illegal taxes. Achebe's reference is intended to recall Cary's irrepressible Mister Johnson, but as 'an intelligent fellow who had been among the first people to receive missionary education in these parts' (*AG* 57). Achebe refuses to substitute a negative stereotype with a positive one. Despite such stories, Ekenzu's village society has remained largely resilient, the majority staunchly upholding Igbo ritual while keeping a distrustful eye on the Christians and their 'new religion'. Unlike Okonkwo for whom Christianity signifies the annihilation of the 'old ways' and the passing of tradition, Ezeulu tries compromise. He sends one of his sons to join the new church in order to understand its potential power. However, compromise is one way in which Ezeulu's standing in the six villages is weakened. The Europeans, no matter how ineffectual they may appear individually, succeed inadvertently in eroding African traditions. The mission church (under the aptly named Mr Goodcountry) slips into the background for most of the novel, but quietly triumphs when the community is persuaded to offer yams for the harvest festival and in so doing discovers an alternative ritual that ensures the late harvesting of their crops. Fear of famine overrules their fear of the external forces and of rituals defiled. In *Things Fall Apart*, a Christian convert kills the clan's sacred python. In *Arrow of God* Ezeulu's son, wary of the python but desperate to prove his scepticism to his new Christian community, imprisons one in a box, knowing it will suffocate but convincing himself that his orchestration of its death is not murder. His action allows Nwaka the leverage he needs to undermine Ezeulu. In both cases, the desecration of a religious symbol precipitates the falling away of the old ways.[9] The more the people listen to Nwaka's republican speeches and fail to allow equal weight for the rites of Ulu, the further Ezeulu shifts towards introspection, stroking his hidden desire to punish rather than cherish.

The erosion of cultural mores that Okonkwo so feared is proved when his death fails to rouse the clan to action against the colonizers on his behalf, even though their insidious presence provoked his final act. He is manhandled even in death by the very interlopers he so despised. In a moment of quiet reflection, Ezeulu reminisces about 'the olden times, when people liked themselves' (*AG* 171) and in his final days he avoids facing the facts that have let the church overtake the Chief Priest. The 'outcome' he avoids is the subject of the novels discussed in the next chapter.

A LANGUAGE OF HIS OWN

Language has been a powerful tool of colonialism. Achebe has been at the forefront of debates about the use of English by Anglophone African writers. The fact that Achebe's fiction has been so acclaimed lies in his manipulation of the English language to recreate Igbo language structures. There are those who assert that the tensions between what African writers want to say and the language they choose to say it led to a diluted sense of African fictional identity. However, Achebe has described literature as 'a veritable weapon' for coping with threats to one's coherent sense of identity. 'Literature as a weapon' is an axiomatic phrase associated more readily with Ngugi Wa Thiong'o than Chinua Achebe. Ngugi's metaphor of 'the barrel of the pen' reflects his rejection of English in favour of his indigenous language, Gikuyu, whereas Achebe's 'African English', it has been argued, inevitably serves less radical purposes. The debate has endured because while the colonizers' language is subordinated through the African writer's economy of representation, the writer continues to appropriate the master's tools to dismantle his house.

Achebe in the now classic statement that 'proverbs are the palm-oil with which words are eaten' (*TFA* 6) succeeds in finding an idiomatic way of expressing the theoretical idea that Mikhail Bakhtin posits: all words have a 'taste'. He suggests that 'Each word tastes of the context and contexts in which it has lived its socially charged life; all words and forms are populated by intentions'.[10] Achebe's English is a hybridized new form of Igbo-English but early debates over his use of language took off in another direction. Early reviewers described *Things Fall Apart* as the first West African novel written in flawless English (clearly a dig at Amos Tutuola's *The Palm-Wine Drinkard*). They praised Achebe's 'brief, almost laconic style' claiming, more effusively, 'Anyone who has read Achebe cannot help but marvel at the way he uses language. He so develops and improvises his medium that one begins to see Nigerian characters talking to each other'.[11] Some reviewers got stuck in a set of assumptions they felt called for them to act as interpreters for the reading public coming to an African story for the first time. Consequently, they take pains to legitimate Achebe's English and to accommodate it, and in so doing fail to recognize what is *different* about it. That Achebe has a facility for using conventional English with confidence is scarcely in doubt. Around the age of 8 Achebe began to learn English formally. In Nigeria, where around 200 languages are spoken, English became not only the language of the colonizer but an educational requirement.[12] Achebe tells stories of finding English the only means to communicate across different linguistic backgrounds. He points us to an inclusive definition of the English language when he talks of pushing back its limits and extending its frontiers.

In borrowing some of the colonialists' resolve, Achebe harnesses the metropolitan language (English in the case of Nigeria) and Western literary traditions for his own artistic, and political purposes. Around the same time, critic of liberation Frantz Fanon also argued that it was possible to reappropriate the language of the colonizer with his example of the French in colonized Algeria. Sartre, in his Introduction to Fanon's *The Wretched of the Earth* (1963), stresses that bending the metropolitan language may achieve revolutionary ideological effects. Fanon and Sartre posited what was revolutionary in turning the tables on the colonizer, utilizing the colonizer's tools against him. In contrast to Conrad's unintelligible Africans, Achebe is renowned for creating orators, characters who are wordsmiths, like Nwaka in *Arrow of God* who is known as 'the Owner of Words'. Nwaka manages to convince his listeners of his point of view and even to follow him over Ezeulu due to his powers of oration. He is reminiscent of Okika in *Things Fall Apart* whose bold words precede Okonkwo's killing of the messenger and could be said to bolster his resolve. The speech he makes is messianic; it is a call to manhood and a blueprint for action. Okika's oratorical skills are those of a preacher who punctuates each carefully-measured phrase with a pause:

> 'My father used to say to me: "Whenever you see a toad jumping in broad daylight, then you know that something is after its life." When I saw you all pouring into this meeting from all the quarters of our clan so early in the morning, I knew that something was after our life. . . . All our gods are weeping. Idemili is weeping. Ogwugwu is weeping, and all the others. Our dead fathers are weeping . . . This is a great gathering. No clan can boast of greater numbers or greater valour. Are all the sons of Umuofia with us here? . . . They are not . . . They have broken the clan and gone their several ways. We who are here this morning have remained true to our fathers . . . We must root out this evil. And if our brothers take the side of evil we must root them out too. And we must do it now. We must bale this water now that it is only ankle-deep . . .' (*TFA* 179)

Okika is interrupted by the messenger and when Okonkwo kills him there is tumult. Despite the clan's shock and surprise, Okika's speech agitates for war. Okika foreshadows another orator, Ikem in *Anthills of the Savannah*, a novel populated by articulate writers and intellectuals. While Ikem's oration has become less dependent on the rich illustrations that proverbs provide, it is one such maxim told to him by an old man that inspires him to make a heartfelt speech, 'The Tortoise and the Leopard – a political meditation on the imperative of struggle', to the 2,000-strong Student Union. It takes up more than a chapter. Proverbs function to illuminate the learned ways of the elders (as Okika uses his) or to signal epiphanies (as with Ikem).

When proverbs are layered, as in the speech of Ezeulu or Nwaka throughout *Arrow of God*, they work cumulatively to penetrate English rhetorical devices and replace them with Igbo speech patterns. This is the cross-fertilization of literacy and orality that so compels Achebe as a writer. The stories that proverbs elicit often prompt laughter but they also contain a hint of iron, although, as he demonstrates in *No Longer at Ease* through Mary's speech, reeling out the proverbs can leave younger acculturated listeners blinking. In fact, the shift to pidgin that occurs most strikingly in *A Man of the People* and *Anthills of the Savannah*, signals the loss of a heightened sense of community as epitomized in the use of proverbs and parables in earlier texts. Pidgin is a language into which Achebe's young and educated characters retreat when they speak to young and uneducated characters or sometimes when there is no language in common. It can be vibrant and it can signal a paucity of speech, but it never has the resonance of Achebe's own brand of Africanized English. Across his work, the relationship between English and Igbo is dialogic; Achebe has often expressed that relationship as a conversation and used metaphors borrowed from music to convey the nuances of Igbo speech. In 2000, in conversation with Toni Morrison, he described the close relationship between sound and meaning in Igbo, a language that he asserts sings to its listeners: 'you can't speak Igbo unless you hear it as music. And I think that's part of my responsibility as a writer, whether I'm writing in English or in Igbo. The tone links prose to poetry, and poetry to music – it's not on the surface, but it's there, embedded in the language itself'.[13]

Okonkwo and Ezeulu set themselves above their peers in a democracy where an individual's leadership is deemed possible only insofar as it represents the group. The hubris inherent in each of Achebe's protagonists varies in degree and according to personality as well as the periods in which they are located. Achebe's works always have a genealogical significance, as I discuss in chapter 4 in specific relation to fathers and sons. It takes half a century for Okonkwo's action to be worked into Igbo history and legend: an Umuofian points out to Nwoye that he should be proud that his son is 'the grandson of Ogbuefi Okonkwo who faced the white man single-handed and died in the fight' (*NLE* 48). Achebe has said more than once that he believes the country of his birth is in great need of reminders; the test of a nation's health is its ability to remember. In *Arrow of God*, for instance, Ezeulu the Chief Priest states that elders such as he should continually enumerate the old ways. For much of the novel he is configured as guardian of those customs that are eroding as the colonial enterprise encroaches on Igbo sytems of tribal organization. In this way the novel echoes *Things Fall Apart*, in which it is made clear that 'an old man was very close to the ancestors' and 'a man's life from birth to death was a series of transition rites which brought him nearer and nearer to his ancestors' (*TFA* 107). Achebe's elders function as carriers of traditions first; they are reservoirs of heritage and history and even though they may be doomed like Okonkwo in *Things Fall Apart* or tested and found wanting like Ezkeulu, their presence is a significant component of Achebe's literary nation-in-the-making.

Achebe presents himself as a liberal humanist who writes in the liberal discourse of rights and representation. He is not comfortable with a socialist literary agenda but continues to focus most of his attention on an educated elite and displays a 'temperate, fine-tuned humanism' according to one reviewer of his essays.[14] He is often compared to African American writers like James Baldwin, who he met and admired, and Toni Morrison with whom he discussed issues of race and representation in a public conversation in 2000.[15] Achebe and Morrison are both acclaimed for having created effective history, endowing the 'unknowable' past with textuality. Morrison's *Song of Solomon* (1977) and the neo-slave narrative *Beloved* (1988) configure this kind of revisionist history. Achebe has asserted that literature is always situated in a particular geopolitical space in that it 'evolves out of the necessities of history, past and current, and the aspirations and destiny of its people' (*MYCD* 7). *Arrow of God* evolves out of a snippet of historical information whereby in 1913 the Chief of the villages of Umuchu in Eastern Nigeria rejected the 'honour' of being made a Warrant Chief, as part of Governor Lugard's system of indirect rule. He was incarcerated for some two months. *Beloved* evolved similarly out of the story of the escaped slave Margaret Garner who made the tragic decision to kill her children rather than have them returned to slavery.[16] Both writers revalorize what Morrison calls 'discredited knowledge', devalued ways of knowing and philosophizing debunked as folk wisdom. Interviewed by Melvyn Bragg on the *South Bank Show* following his delivery of the South Bank lecture on 'African Literature as Restoration of Celebration', Achebe asserted that the absence of speech in the portrayal of Africans in colonial fiction was a component of the 'alibi' put together by those committing the twin crimes of plunder and subjugation.[17] Revisionist writing seeks to demolish that alibi.

In Achebe's fiction the past functions as a reservoir from which rituals and stories submerged in the period of colonialization may be reaccentuated. Rituals change and develop as generations debate their centrality as social functions. In Achebe's fictions they are often the site over which two generations of male characters struggle. As the chapter that follows will show, despite the increasing heterogeneity of Nigerian nationhood, the tensions inherent in regionalism and tribalism persist past Independence celebrations. As Benedict Anderson points out, 'nationalism was then thinly enough spread in Nigeria' for the military coup in January of 1966 to be recast as an Igbo plot.[18] Subsequent anti-Igbo feeling and repercussions led to civil war and the secession of Biafra. Ethnic rivalry, group rituals and even the myths that emerged out of precolonial lifestyles could prove sources of tension for the new nation.

4

Politicians, Pioneers, Prodigal Sons: *No Longer at Ease* and *A Man of the People*

Vote for the car and you will ride in it!

> (Chinua Achebe, 'The Voter', 1965,
> in *Girls at War and Other Stories*, 1972)

What is a pioneer? Someone who shows the way. That is what I am doing.

> (Obi Okonkwo in Chinua Achebe,
> *No Longer at Ease*, 1960)

... the village had a mind; it could say no to sacrilege. But in the affairs of the nation ... the laws of the village became powerless.

> (Chinua Achebe, *A Man of the People*, 1966)

It has become axiomatic that anti-colonial struggles produce neocolonial conditions. Achebe's critique of the emergent African nation-state in *No Longer at Ease* and *A Man of the People* is a closely observed, dystopian depiction of the internal conflicts that would split Nigeria by the end of the 1960s. In his second and fourth novels, Achebe mounts a biting critique of the new black bourgeoisie and of totalitarian regimes, whether civilian or military. *No Longer at Ease* strikes a cautionary note pre-Independence and *A Man of the People* provides a satirical spin on post-Independence government practices. From *Things Fall Apart*, recovering the historical past has become a ubiquitous theme for Achebe. In these novels it remains a social blueprint as it becomes clear that the national experience is condensed into plot at the level of individual characters, 'new' Nigerians in the 'new' nation. In *No Longer at Ease* and *A Man of the People*, Obi Okonkwo and Odili Samalu are representative of the fatal flaws in their nation's political make-up; in the neocolonial and postcolonial eras new capitalism has fostered apathetic individuals. The knot that ties each of them to family and community – Obi to Umuofia and Odili to Urua, a village outside Anata – loosens as each drifts into a narcissistic lifestyle and a form of cultural liminality. Obi reads his own life as a kind of literary exegesis, interpreting each situation according to the European and usually modernist literature he studied at university. Odili tries to make sense of the mid-1960s by telling his story retrospectively and discovers in the process that there are no heroes involved, not even himself. By the end of the novel, he has returned home armed with a stronger sense of self and community.

Ruling military juntas have elevated one ethnic group while targeting another at different turning points in Nigeria's bloody and uneven history. Igbo and Ogoni peoples, for example, have each undergone vigorous internal controls and found themselves the subject of discussion in the international community. In the literary world, the murder of Ken Saro-Wiwa, hanged by General Sani Abacha in 1995 for fighting for Ogoni rights, is a tragic case in point. His *Sozaboy: A Novel in Rotten English* (1985) remains one of the best-known portraits of Nigerian corruption. He protested the London oil company Shell International's destruction of Ogoni land in Eastern Nigeria ('The flames of Shell are flames of hell / We bake beneath their light') and gave up an academic life to fight the Ogoni cause. In 1993, and again in 1994, Saro-Wiwa, as President of the Movement for the Survival of the Ogoni People, was imprisoned. In a rigged trial, the peaceful campaigner stood accused of the murder of other Ogoni leaders, a charge he always denied. His execution took place, despite international pressure, in November of 1995. The hanging was botched more than once, during which time Saro-Wiwa's last public words are reported to have been, 'Why are you people doing this to me? What kind of nation is this?' Following Saro-Wiwa's death, Soyinka described Abacha as a 'psychopathic' leader of a 'murdering cabal'.[1] Nigeria has become best known as a country broken by ethnic factions, a kleptocracy looted by despotic leaders time and again over the forty-year history of its independence. The same general who hanged Saro-Wiwa is now known to have ripped off his country's Central Bank for around £2 billion during his stint in power. An infamous succession of civil and military governments and the accompanying atrocities of their regimes have contributed to the despoilation of the nation and to its poor reputation in international circles, as I go on to discuss in chapter 5.

Although much of what has occurred in Nigeria is tragic, in *No Longer at Ease* and *A Man of the People* Achebe begins to expose what began as a national farce – with fear at its edges. In *A Man of the People* a government minister fears he has been poisoned by his political rivals, but it transpires that the bitter taste in his coffee results from the fact that it is produced locally, rather than the smooth foreign brand he usually drinks. The government launches a campaign known as OHMS (Our Home Made Stuff) to persuade Nigerians to consume locally made products while government ministers continue to drink Nescafé and import clothes made of pure English wool. In *The Condition of Postmodernity* (1989), David Harvey examines the 'free' market trading that reduces the world's geography to commodities. The beginnings of a commodity culture have been seen by many, usually Marxist, theorists as the basis for cultural amnesia, the kind of forgetting that leads to social alienation. Achebe's protagonists are caught in a liminal space between a communal past and a turbulent present in which they can find no secure foothold except in materialism.

No Longer at Ease opens and closes with the trial of Okonkwo's grandson. The trial is a trope to which Achebe returns in *Anthills of the Savannah*, where a leader and a country are put on trial. Here it frames the narrative, but Obi has not committed a heinous violation: he has slowly succumbed to petty crime. Obi is a young civil servant who has accepted bribes of sex or money to facilitate educational scholarships. His crime is an infraction against the Umuofian clan who paid for his education in England, and who elevated him as their representative in 'the vanguard' of the colonial administration, as it gives way to the new metropolitan regime in the years preceding Independence. As a bright English graduate being interviewed for his post in the civil service, Obi is self-righteously shocked when asked whether he may be predisposed to accept bribes from the public, yet Achebe ensures that this is exactly what he does: 'Everybody wondered why. The learned judge . . . could not comprehend how an educated man and so on and so forth' (*NLE* 154). Obi, like Cary's Mister Johnson is a spendthrift who becomes disfigured by an apathetic materialism: he desires all the trappings of his success and fails to budget for them. Finally, he drifts into accepting bribes and is arrested. Achebe withholds the 'ending' of the novel. Obi's life as he has come to know it in Lagos is ended: he is estranged from his father, his mother has died, and his girlfriend, Clara, has left him and aborted their child, a decision Obi greets in terms of finance rather than feeling. But the reader is encouraged to read beyond the 'ending' of his trial. There is no 'merciful' Rudbeck to put Obi out of his misery. His boss, Mr Green, is too bitter about the end of empire to mourn a colonial subject's fall at the onset of Independence. Obi is convicted of bribery by the outgoing colonial regime when incoming governments, like the one depicted in *A Man of the People* will make bribery a mainstay of their administrations. In *No Longer at Ease* it is the 'people's business to get as much from [the government] as they could without getting into trouble' (*NLE* 33) but in *A Man of the People*, set only a few years later, the government siphons off money from the people's coffers. Seats in parliament are bought, Minister Nanga can control the press with a 'dash' of five pounds here and there, and the country's trade is fixed by pay-offs.

Achebe has often described *A Man of the People* as a 'serious indictment' of post-Independence Nigeria but it is also a searing and often very funny farce. It is the story of the rise and fall of Chief Nanga, a man of the people who has risen from schoolmaster to Minister for Culture in a corrupt civilian government. The narrator, Odili, is a bright and very average young man who sneers at Nanga, his former teacher, but is quickly seduced by the minister's wealth and poise. Flattered by his attention, he seeks to emulate the older man but is personally betrayed when Nanga seduces his girlfriend, Elsie.

He turns his attentions to Edna, the young lady Nanga has earmarked to be his second 'parlour' wife. Odili comes to his political senses but his motives are a jumble of ambition and revenge. Persuaded by his activist friend Max, he tries to stand against Nanga in the election that takes place at the end of the novel, knowing that he will fail and that the election will be rigged. Odili is physically assaulted on Nanga's election platform (literally when he attends a Nanga rally) and wakes up in hospital with a cracked skull and other injuries. Odili's ethics are twisted back into shape by the experience, but he discovers Max has been murdered. In the last pages of the novel a military coup rids the country of its corrupt leadership and Odili marries Edna, the girl he has come to love, having 'saved' her from becoming Nanga's second wife.

Achebe's satire is at its most pronounced in *A Man of the People*: 'the great collusive swindle that was independence started to show its true face to us' (*HI* 58). Achebe remembers the wife of a British diplomat who proclaimed herself 'aghast' at his 'disservice' to his country by writing this novel (*HI* 50). General definitions of satire presuppose that what is depicted will be exaggerated in order to act as a chilling warning of what might ensue, like Huxley's *Brave New World* or Orwell's *Nineteen Eighty-Four*. However, Achebe stays so close to the mood of the country in *A Man of the People* that on publication there were even rumours that he had engineered the coup that took place in the week his novel was published. Although *A Man of the People* has been read as prophetic, it would be more accurate to say that it is an uncannily vivid political fable. It is a 'condition-of-Nigeria' novel and a strike against the cynicism of a nation that fails to hold unscrupulous politicians accountable.

RETURN OF THE PRODIGAL

Obi is a 'been-to': he has 'been to' England and returns empowered with the same knowledge that authorized the colonialists. Returning to Umuofia, he is revered as the prodigal son; the citizens of Umuofia have taxed themselves in order to pay to send their brightest child to England for the kind of education that will ensure him a post in Nigeria's civil service and their country's administration on his return. The Secretary of the Umuofia Progressive Union (UPU) speaks emphatically of 'the importance of having one of our sons in the vanguard of this march of progress' before going on to state, rather more obliquely, the expectations all Umuofians have of Obi:

> Our people have a saying 'Ours is ours, but mine is mine'. Every town and village struggles at this momentous epoch in our political evolution to possess that of which it can say: 'This is mine'. We are happy that today we have such an invaluable possession in the person of our illustrious son and guest of honour. (*NLE* 32)

Though veiled by abstraction the elevation of the collective over individual ambition is clear: Obi is bought and paid for.

Obi is sent to England with a view to become a lawyer, a profession that has practical values in that he may help his people settle land disputes. However, Obi, in his individuality, opts to study English, a subject seemingly without any intrinsic value for nation-building. This is his first act of rebellion, the assertion of his individuality in contrast to the communal subject position expected of him by the elders. Obi and his community are caught in the maelstrom of modernizing forces in the soon-to-be independent Nigeria, whilst adhering to traditional values which have become tempered by the popularity of Christianity. The following speech delivered as Obi sets out to fulfil their hopes in England illustrates this well:

> 'Umuofia would have required you to fight in her wars and bring home human heads. But those were days of darkness from which we have been delivered by the blood of the Lamb of God. Today we send you to bring knowledge. Remember that the fear of the Lord is the beginning of wisdom. I have heard of young men from other towns who went to the white man's country, but instead of facing their studies they went after the sweet things of the flesh. Some of them even married white women.' The crowd murmured its strong disapproval of such behaviour. 'A man who does that is lost to his people. He is like rain wasted in the forest ... We are sending you to learn book. Enjoyment can wait. Do not be in a hurry to rush into the pleasures of the world like the young antelope who danced herself lame when the main dance was yet to come.' ...

61

The gathering ended with the singing of 'Praise God from whom all blessings flow.' The guests ... shook hands with him and as they did so they pressed their presents into his palm, to buy a pencil with, or an exercise book or a loaf of bread for the journey, a shilling there and a penny there – substantial presents in a village where money was so rare, where men and women toiled from year to year to wrest a meagre living from an unwilling and exhausted soil. (*NLE* 10–12)

The entanglement of Igbo proverbs and Christian hymns in this excerpt epitomizes the potential for an alliance between the traditional and modern, but also contained within the passage is the inexorable tension between the two. In order to send Obi to England the people have had to tax themselves, despite their poor incomes, and expect him to repay their efforts both in material terms and through his actions on their behalf.

Initially at least, the Umuofians have little cause to worry: Obi is not seduced by England the country, despite spending four years there; on the contrary, his 'longing to return home took on the sharpness of physical pain' (*NLE* 13). His experiences away from home also bring him to the realization that Nigeria is more than simply a name, but from a distance he concocts a romanticized version of the country. He composes poems:

> God bless our noble fatherland,
> Great land of sunshine bright,
> Where brave men chose the way of peace,
> To win their freedom fight.
> May we preserve our purity,
> Our zest for life and jollity.
>
> God bless our noble countrymen
> And women everywhere.
> Teach them to walk in unity
> To build our nation dear:
> Forgetting region, tribe or speech.
> But caring always each for each.

(*NLE* 103)

In its sentimental, lyrical approach Obi's poem betrays a number of paradoxes. The truly brave men – like his grandfather Okonkwo – did not choose the way of peace in their freedom fight. Obi's generation cannot remember a time when Nigeria was without a controlling white presence. The line 'May we preserve our purity' betrays a monologic outlook, clearly without compromise or understanding, and yet the poem urges Nigerians to forget region, tribe and language. While the reader cringes at the naïvety of the poem he entitles 'Nigeria', when Obi returns to the poem some while after its composition he smiles indulgently.

Obi becomes the Umuofians' educated representative in Lagos and unlike other city-living Umuofians eking out a living as taxi drivers or stall holders, Obi earns as much in a month as they do in a year. His neocolonial cultural capital is further enhanced by a beautiful 'been-to' girlfriend, but begins to lapse when he proves to the UPU that he is incapable of living within his quite considerable means. They also discover that Clara, his 'intended', is *osu*, an outcast whose family was dedicated to the gods and who will be considered lowly and degenerate, as will their children as long as clan lore persists. Obi and Clara are presented as a bright, educated couple in the vanguard of the 'new nation'. They are failed precursors to Chris and Beatrice in *Anthills of the Savannah* since, unlike the couple in the 1980s, they make scant attempt to engage with the possibilities inherent in self-rule, other than their new-found material wealth at the end of the 1950s:

'This is a wonderful day,' he told Clara on the telephone. 'I have sixty pounds in my pocket, and I'm getting my car at two o'clock.' Clara screamed with delight. (*NLE* 60)

Obi engages a driver and they drive twelve miles in his Morris Oxford for a celebratory meal, but even the trappings of materialism fail to cushion their relationship: it is on this evening that Clara tells Obi she is an *osu*. As soon as difficulties begin to surface that demand committed action on Obi's part, he starts to fade. Obi's betrayal of Clara contrasts with Amos, in the 1960 short story 'Chike's School Days', who marries an *osu* despite opposition: 'But then Amos was nothing if not mad. The new religion had gone to his head. It was like palm-wine. Some people drank it and remained sensible. Others lost every sense in their stomach' (*GW* 36). Obi colludes in that facet of colonial discourse that presents him as national and moral minor – former colonized subjects are never culpable because never capable. He is incredibly naïve on so many occasions: he is surprised to discover that the salary he earns will be taxed, and shocked that the electricity he consumes should involve him in significant expense, namely household bills.

Obi is Achebe's first detailed attempt at portraying the effects and consequences of direct cultural exchange between Nigerians and Europeans. In *Things Fall Apart*, Achebe's African translators function in a marginal manner, as interlocutors for the European paymasters. Those Umuofians who convert to Christianity tend to be village outcasts and undeserving of narrative development in what is, after all, Okonkwo's story. However, in *No Longer at Ease* a culturally hybridized Nigerian is the protagonist. Much has been made of the positive effects of hybridity by postcolonial critics,[2] but for Achebe hybridity is neither an answer to nor a solution for the psychological effects of colonization for someone like Obi. Mr Green – like the District Commissioner in *Things Fall Apart* – holds an essentialized view of the people among whom he lives and works. In a revealing conversation at his Club, he has the following to say about Africans:

> The African is corrupt through and through ... They are all corrupt ... The fact that over countless centuries the African has been the victim of the worst climate in the world and every imaginable disease. Hardly his fault. But he has been sapped mentally and physically. We brought him Western education. But what use is it to him? (*NLE* 3)

For Green, racial and ethnic identity is fixed and there is no possibility for change, and Obi does not seek to challenge Green's discourse, 'Our people have a long way to go' (*NLE* 62). In a scene in which he travels in a 'mammy wagon' to visit his family, Obi cogitates on his travelling companions:

> What an Augean stable! He muttered to himself. 'Where does one begin? With the masses? Educate the masses?' He shook his head. 'Not a chance there. It would take centuries. A handful of men at the top. Or even one man with vision – an enlightened dictator. People are scared of the word nowadays. But what kind of

democracy can exist side by side with so much corruption and ignorance? Perhaps a half-way house – a sort of compromise'. (*NLE* 40)

Typically, Obi disdains from thinking further: 'He was not really in the mood for consecutive reasoning' (*NLE* 40). Achebe has Obi echo his boss Mr Green and, in a novel that turns on epistemological uncertainty, Obi remains unequipped to allow thoughts of the 'new nation' to wander too far from what anchors him to European ways of knowing.

Obi's hybridization remains dependent on European mores and European acceptance and the subjugation of his Igbo roots. He has not succeeded in managing the connections between two cultures to fashion himself into a 'new man' by integrating his past with his present. Benedict Anderson, in *Imagined Communities: Reflections on the Origin and Spread of Nationalism* (1983), explains that the nationalism of newly independent nations was based on European ideas of nation that were already a century old. Postcolonial notions of nationhood based on sovereign states fail to transcend the pitfalls bequeathed to them, as Obi fails to transcend his conviction that his European education will shield him at home ('To occupy a "European post" was second only to being a European. It raised a man from the masses to the elite', *NLE* 84).

Frantz Fanon describes the kind of cultural dislocation Obi exemplifies at the end of British rule in *Black Skins, White Masks* (1952), where he speaks of 'individuals without an anchor, without horizon, colourless, stateless, rootless'. And, in *The Wretched of the Earth* (1963), he extrapolates on the process by which the intrinsic identity of colonial subjects is abrogated:

> It is a systematic negation of the other person and a furious determination to deny the other person all attributes of humanity, colonialism forces the people it dominates to ask themselves the question constantly: 'In reality, who am I?'[3]

A psychiatrist, Fanon presented case studies of colonial subjects under French rule in Algeria in order to construct a theory of the psychology of the oppressed that would be political as well as psychological. Obi lacks agency beyond his idea of himself as an educated individual. At his trial the public sees only the moral turpitude of a torpid young man who barely reacts, 'a modern driftwood, manipulated by events and making never a show of resistance' as Soyinka describes his listlessness.[4] Only the tears he cries as the novel opens belie the emotional force with which events have hit Obi. He is alone because he would not commit to anything or anyone, not the Umuofians to whom he is responsible and, least of all, the possibilities for the new Independent and *African* Nigeria.

Obi's dilemma is reflected in the novel's form. In *No Longer at Ease* Achebe begins to depart from the characteristic conventions of literary realism so successful in conveying the lost world of *Things Fall Apart* and *Arrow of God*. He forgoes the archaeological coherence of recuperative history and the project of dis-identification whereby derogatory images of oneself are acted upon and transmogrified.[5] *No Longer at Ease* opens in the present and returns to the recent past before concluding in the present. At one level, the refusal of teleology undermines the efficient linearity of official discourse in the colonial administration system in which Obi has come to work. At another level, and more importantly, the shift in temporality allows Achebe to place the reader in the gallery of the court, where Obi is standing trial for accepting bribes, to actively participate in judging his crime. Achebe reneges on the reader's expectations of a framed narrative where the court, in deciding Obi's fate after the 'evidence' relayed in the novel, pronounces on cause and effect. The novel is contemporaneous with events in Nigeria and these do not coalesce into a coherent framework. Consequently, the novel has what Simon Gikandi calls 'improvisorial elements' in its modes of representation.[6] Not all of Achebe's reviewers welcomed his inventiveness, many preferring the chronological structuring of the earlier work to an experiment in writing contemporaneously. In fact, *No Longer at Ease* has sometimes been deemed the least satisfactory of Achebe's novels due to its lack of clear resolution. A prime example of such criticism is Eustace Palmer, who finds the novel 'greatly inferior' in range of conception and 'intensity of realization'.[7] Readers who invest in a coherent sense of an ending will be disappointed when they find themselves returned in the final paragraph of the novel to the question that Achebe leaves unresolved: why would such an idealistic young man as Obi fall prey to the very temptations that have filled him with contempt for most of the novel.

THE NEOCOLONIAL CONDITION

Obi exists in the precipitous moments of the end of empire in Nigeria. Colonial practices are experienced by colonized subjects as material and psychological violence, bound up in economic realities. As empire recedes, the Umuofians feel they need to make inroads into a national community from which they have been excluded. The Men of the Umuofia Progressive Union describe themselves as 'pioneers' on more than one occasion in *No Longer at Ease*. Their president in Lagos explains to Obi that 'We cannot afford bad ways [because] . . . we are pioneers building up our families and our town' (*NLE* 75), and a friend warns him that his behaviour reflects on the group: 'If one finger brings oil it soils the others [because] . . . we of this generation are only pioneers' (*NLE* 68). Obi fails to walk the path laid out for him as a pioneer for the new nation at the end of the 1950s. He is self-seeking and sluggish rather than forward-looking. In *Arrow of God*, Ezeulu tells his son Odouche that 'The world is like a Mask dancing. If you want to see it well you do not stand in one place' (*AG* 45). Obi is short-sighted, and standing still is no bulwark against the onslaught of change the Umuofians fear.

Where Okonkwo and Ezeulu's tragedies take on epic proportions in the precolonial context of change, Obi's fall from grace is made sadly ironic. His full name, Obiajulu, means 'the mind at last is at rest' but in a modern, ironic 'tragedy' there is no catharsis, release or rest. Borrowing his thesis from W. H. Auden's 'Musée des Beaux Arts' and Graham Greene's *The Heart of the Matter*, Obi relaxes into a short lecture on 'real tragedy' during his job interview and prides himself on discerning that tragedy takes place 'in a corner, an untidy spot' and is never resolved. Achebe lets him fulfil his own prophesy but withholds judgement on the moment at which 'the rains break' for Obi. Instead, he juxtaposes fragmented scenes in which Clara terminates their child and he fails to act; and he shreds the poem 'Nigeria' on which he looked so indulgently;

and he is taunted with being a 'beast of no nation' when he jumps the queue at the hospital where Clara lies ill (*NLE* 135–8). Similarly, the moment at which he accepts the bribes that condemn him is equally murky: sex with a schoolgirl is a blur against the beat of 'high life' music, and the money is accepted in equally ambiguous circumstances.

Obi falls into a personality trap that Achebe equates with a neocolonial disease, 'the near pathological eagerness to contract the sicknesses of Europe in the horribly mistaken belief that our claim to sophistication is improved thereby' (*MYCD* 24). Obi filters each aspect of his life through a European lens so that any self-searching involves only the extent to which he mirrors his European counterparts. Achebe reworks Cary's acculturated Africans, like Louis Aladai in *The African Witch*, who dismisses his own cultural background, basing his decision on European art and letters rather than his knowledge of colonial history. As discussed in chapter 2, Achebe refuses to produce fictions that counter derogatory depictions of Africans during the colonial period with positive images of shining paragons. Colonized subjects like Obi have internalized colonial systems and values through a series of cultural practices that they live out in the neocolonial phase of self-goverment,[8] as an uncharacteristically decisive Obi tells Mr Green:

> 'You devised these soft conditions for yourselves when every European was automatically in the senior service and every African automatically in the junior service. Now that a few of us have been admitted into the senior service, you turn around and blame us'. (*NLE* 140)

Obi is caught between the pretensions of urban success and the pressures of filial and familial duty, but the one overrides the other. He believes the chief crisis he suffers is financial: when he examines 'the mainspring of his actions' it is to his finances he turns, even before Clara, who spends five weeks hospitalized following the termination. In a 1964 essay, Achebe alleges: 'Today we have kept the materialism and thrown away the spirituality that should keep it in check.'[9] The question of balance/imbalance that underpins *Things Fall Apart* is explored to more disturbing effect in *No Longer at Ease*. Once again Achebe borrows ironically from Western poetic discourse, taking his title from T. S. Eliot's poem 'The Journey of the Magi', which also serves to provide the book with its epigraph:

> We returned to our places, these Kingdoms,
> But no longer at ease here, in the old dispensation,
> With an alien people clutching their gods.
> I should be glad of another death.

Obi is a man of two worlds in a society in transition. This is played out in the text in the journeys Obi takes and in the overall movement from country to city.[10] The city has become acculturated: expensive restaurants disdain to sell Nigerian food, for example. In one short scene Obi visits a supposedly swish restaurant owned by an elderly Englishwoman whose favourite spot is the table beneath her parrot's cage: 'As soon as she sat down the parrot emerged from its cage on to a projecting rod, lowered its tail, and passed ordure, which missed the old lady by a tenth of an inch . . . But there was no mess. Everything was beautifully organized. There was a tray by the old lady's chair nearly full of wet excrement' (*NLE* 31). Through such scenes Achebe charts cultural loss and stagnation.

Lagos is sharply divided into zones according to race and class divisions. Obi rarely leaves the suburb in which bright young civil servants are expected to live. Therefore, the sequence in which Obi drives Clara to her seamstress's house is unusual in that it takes in the Lagos slums. Obi waits for her by a meat stall that stands close to a 'wide-open storm drain from which came a very strong smell of rotting flesh' (the remains of a dead dog). He watches a boy selling bean cakes engaged in a jokey altercation with a 'night-soilman' passing by 'trailing clouds of putrefaction'. Musing on the scene, Obi juxtaposes it with one of his own 'callow' poems about 'sweet' Nigeria. He is struck by the irony, but instead of coming to consciousness that 'sweet Nigeria' cannot be made in England and that social programmes must clean up the mess the colonizers will leave behind, he contrives another quotation. 'I have tasted putrid flesh in the spoon' is presumably Obi's effort to invoke T. S. Eliot's 'Prufrock' and the 'measuring out' of life 'in coffee spoons' (*NLE* 14). On the way home Obi almost kills a cyclist with 'Future Minister' on his bicycle bag. But he returns quietly to his flat in a 'European reserve' that is blank, white and banal. Obi knows none of his neighbours and, once he has given up visiting his friend Joseph, he is completely without community. The narrator's image of twin kernels of a palm-nut shell, one 'shiny-black and alive, the other powdery-white and dead' (*NLE* 16) is presented to the reader as more apt and evocative of his situation than Obi's obscure posturing. Scatological motifs are taken up again in *A Man of the People* via descriptions of city plumbing: in the *Daily Chronicle*, residents are reminded of a 1951 'Bye-law' which limits the number and type of pails provided for excrement in each home. As Odili reads, he muses on the differences between pit latrines and bucket latrines as he luxuriates in Nanga's mansion home with the seven 'gleaming, silent action' water closets. Just a few years after the period described in *No Longer at Ease*, the city is sinking into the sewer, the cesspool of misrule that is the 'new nation'.

FATHERS AND SONS

Discussing his own family background, Achebe confides that there was always a feeling between his father and great-grandfather that he found 'moving and perplexing'. The novel that is 'missing' from what Achebe has sometimes referred to as 'the Okonkwo trilogy' perhaps remains unwritten because his father's parents died young and in his 'gallery of ancestral heroes' there is a space that he has refrained from filling with his imaginings (*MYCD* 67). However, the tension between fathers and sons is a recurring motif in Achebe's fiction. In *Arrow of God*, Egogo, Ezeulu's eldest son, complains that his father's paternalism is confining: 'He must go on treating his grown children like little boys . . . the older his children grew the more he seemed to dislike them' (*AG* 91). Ezeulu finds it easier to chide his sons than to commend them, and Akuebue quietly takes him to task for underestimating Egogo and for chastizing Obika for his altercation with Mr Clarke before he has heard his side of the story. The archetypal tension is residual resentment that Okonkwo feels for his father even ten years after his death. In *Things Fall Apart* and *Arrow of God* tensions derive from precolonial definitions of manhood and from fathers responding differently to children they have with different wives. The tensions become less clearly defined as the generations pass.

The effects of colonialism are responded to differently by each generation of Okonkwo men. In *No Longer at Ease*: 'The second generation of educated Nigerians had gone back to eating pounded yams or *garri* with their fingers for the good reason that it tasted better that way. Also for the even better reason that they were not as scared as the first generation of being called uncivilized'. (*NLE* 18) The intertextual relationship between Achebe's first novel and *No Longer at Ease* is explicatory of the kinds of cross-generational tensions that fuel misunderstandings and resentments. Okonkwo and his grandson Obi live symbolically parallel lives ('he is Ogbuefi Okonkwo come back', *NLE* 56), but there is little real symmetry. The fall of Okonkwo's grandson is not the result of having acted on what he believes to be right. The book's central themes are cultural alienation and corruption as bound up in the dialectical relationship between collectivity and autonomy, colonial rule and Independence. Obi believes that a new Nigeria will emerge once the older generation of Africans leaves the young and educated space to create it, but by *A Man of the People* the men from the universities are the 'Miscreant Gang' dismissed in favour of Nanga's party.

Obi may more usefully be compared with his father because Achebe patterns three lives into a web of similar concerns, each man reacting against his father and doubting his son. As Okonkwo resents Unoka's 'femininity', so he curses his son Nwoye when – newly christened Isaac – he turns away from his father in turning towards Christianity. In *No Longer at Ease* Achebe takes Nwoye back to the scene in *Things Fall Apart* when he realizes that his father has killed his playmate and adopted brother and 'something seemed to give way inside him, like the snapping of a tightened bow. He did not cry. He just hung limp' (*TFA* 54). The image of a warrior's bow snapping is a simple yet evocative one; Nwoye rejects the clan's customs and becomes Isaac. He remembers one other occasion when he learned that twins were left to die in the Evil Forest according to clan lore; the sound of an infant crying in the forest provokes a similar visceral reaction in the boy. No longer a young son, but a retired catechist at the end of his life, Isaac still smarts at the memories, resenting his father for Ikefuma's death half a century later: 'those who kill by the machet must die by the machet'. When Obi seems to react listlessly to news of his mother's death, other Umuofians pronounce him his father's son. Achebe makes it clear that a son can scarcely avoid some resemblance to his father. In fact, when Isaac rejects Obi's choice of marriage partner, citing the clan lore he has excised from his own life, he echoes his own father's dismissal of his life choices.

Each man in his own way offends the Umuofian clan, rejects Igbo beliefs and is made vulnerable by his displacement. However, as Achebe shows through *Things Fall Apart* and *Arrow of God*, the clan is not a monolithic structure. By the 1950s, Okonkwo has been returned to the pantheon of the clan's 'great men' and his is among the names that Odogwu recites to convince Obi that, although these men were 'great in their day', 'Today greatness has changed its tune. Titles are no longer great, neither are barns or large numbers of wives and children. Greatness is now in the things of white men. And so we have changed our tune' (*NLE* 49). This is precisely why the loss of Obi is not mourned as tragic in the way of Okonkwo but as part of an inevitable erosion of character that is the by-product of neocolonialism. Achebe characterizes the generations as 'defectors and loyalists' (*HI* 22), but what they defect *from* changes with each generation. Obi returns from England as a lapsed Christian: he no longer believes in 'the father's God' (*NLE* 51). This change is reflected in his favourite poem, A. E. Housman's 'Easter Hymn', an atheist exposé of Christian hope, but he cannot tell his father even though he knows his mother has espoused Igbo traditions and stories in clandestine fashion for all the years of their marriage.

Where Obi is denied the prodigal's final escape route back to Umuofia, Odili returns to his village, to his father and to ritual – his wedding. Only Odili in *A Man of the People* succeeds in being reconciled with the father he has derided and whose counsel he has failed to heed. By the end of the novel, they are sustaining one another in a political stance against corrupt practices. Odili's father is his main support:

I thought to myself: You do not belong to this age, old man. Men of worth nowadays simply forget what they said yesterday. Then I realized that I had never really been close enough to my father to understand him. I had built up a private picture of him from unconnected scraps of evidence. (*MP* 135)

Although Achebe stops his narrator in his tracks ('Anyway, this was no time to begin a new assessment; it was better left to the tax people'), it is in the most comical and satirical of the tales he tells that the father/son relationship becomes any-where near mutual respect.

SLICING THE NATIONAL CAKE

A Man of the People reworks the short story 'The Voter' with its rigged election battle between two parties called POP and PAP and the protagonist casting his vote for both of them in the same ballot box. In *A Man of the People* POP and PAP have an equally murky history, 'as when a few years ago ten newly elected P.A.P. Members of Parliament had switched parties at the opening of the session and given the P.O.P. a comfortable majority overnight in return for ministerial appointments and – if one believed in rumours – a little cash prize as well' (*MP* 82). Nanga's POP is challenged by a new party, Odili and Max's own CPC or the Common People's Convention. Achebe shows that there is little hope of vying for public opinion when the electorate can be bribed and that in the farcical game of politics it is not finally the people who topple governments. At the end of the novel, POP is brought down by a coup, 'unruly mobs and private armies having tasted blood and power during the election . . . they had no public reason for doing it. Let's make no mistake about that'. By the end of the novel, Odili's eyes are wide open politically. All moves in the political game are driven by the power of the ubiquitous phrase 'getting a slice of the national cake' (or 'national loot' as Achebe terms it in *The Trouble with Nigeria*).

Chief the Honourable M. A. Nanga is taken to the hearts of his constituents in Anata when he pays what Achebe condemns elsewhere as a 'siren-visit' (*TN* 24), full of smiles and promises and over-brimming with the rhetoric of local factionalism. He winningly declares he was never happier than when he worked as a teacher at the local school and avows that 'we shouldn't leave everything to the highland tribes', because 'our people' should be pressing for a significant slice of the national cake (*MP* 12). Odili, scrutinizing this so-called 'man of the people', is not initially impressed. Like Obi, he has a young man's developed sense of self-righteous indignation and a fairly developed sense of his own educated abilities. But, unlike Obi, Odili has a burgeoning political sense of 'the nation's system of choosing and rewarding its hierarchy of public servants', something Achebe denounces elsewhere as 'the real explosive potential of social injustice in Nigeria' insofar as it creates the 'gargantuan disparity of privilege' of a tiny elite over the mass populace (*TN* 22). Odili remembers the conspiracies that brought his former teacher to power and itches to renounce him publicly, but Achebe first ensures that his head is turned by the same materialism that seduced the teacher into politics, when he spends time in Nanga's house as a general factotum.

Achebe's fourth novel revels in the kind of incisive and dry wit that he used to more guarded effect in *No Longer at Ease*. Where the former includes a few short satirical scenes (as a small boy a misguided Obi wrote a letter to Hitler because he felt sorry for him), Achebe makes it clear in *A Man of the People* that the responsibility for the nation's progress is bound up in each individual act, no matter how outlandish. Even Chief the Honourable Nanga's title is a pretentious messy hybrid that oozes self-importance and impacts on those around him: he even seduces the 'Ego Women's Party' into offering him unqualified support. The parties Odili attends and the individuals he encounters all lend something to the general mêlée that is Nigerian politics. For example, a satirical subtext is the exposé of the links between cultural imperialism and global capitalism, most specifically the financial relationship between Nigeria and America, from the concrete – American capital finances a new cement factory! – to the more esoteric – a team of American 'experts' has been employed to advise Nigeria on how to improve its public image in America. The latter example is comically unpacked at a soirée at which one of the experts working for the transnational corporation, secure in his new Nigerian market, pronounces on the faults of the country. The American uses his own nation's history of lynching as a barometer of social progress: lynching did not begin as a racist ritual and over the last ten years lynchings have occurred in only five of them! Ironies abound in such twisted logic and, although 'America may not be perfect', he cautions any one who might doubt its proximity to perfection: 'but don't forget that we are the only powerful country in the entire history of the world, the only one, which had the power to conquer others and didn't do it. ... Perhaps we are naïve. We still believe in such outdated concepts like freedom, like letting every man run his show. Americans have never wished to be involved in anyone else's show ...' (*MP* 45). Achebe lets the garrulous (and mistaken) American drift off unchecked. Odili's shock is left unspoken on this occasion.

Although the political chicanery threaded through *A Man of the People* promotes as much levity as thought, the ideals of the young Nigerians are trounced when Max is assassinated. Fear of violence and its expression is always on the edges of the humour in the second half of the novel. Odili even has to engage a set of bodyguards once his determination to stand as Nanga's political opponent is announced, and they carry five machetes, empty bottles and stones in the boot of their election car: 'Later we were compelled to add two double-barrelled guns ... after many acts of violence were staged against us ... Their declared aim was to "annihilate all enemies of progress" and "to project true Nangaism" ' (*MP* 112). Odili even becomes quite jubilant when he sees his name on placards like 'NANGAISM FOREVER: SAMALU IS TREITOR', and is in danger of getting carried away by his own campaign. Achebe's headstrong protagonists usually have a friend who speaks the truth but whose advice is ignored: Oberika functions in this way for Okonkwo in *Things Fall Apart* and Akuebue is 'one of the very few men of Umuaro whose words gained entrance into Ezeulu's ear' (*AG* 93). Odili has had Max as confidant but also as challenger, the force behind his commitment to political change. Max's betrayal by accepting money from a minister, even though he uses it to the CPC's advantage, unsettles their association, but, after Max is dead, Odili locates his mistake in a context he can live with. Max's death provokes one of the very few scenes of genuine emotion in the novel and it is simply and cleanly evoked: 'I wept all day that day, and the pressure inside my head returned and I hoped I would die, but the doctor put me to sleep' (*MP* 142).

Betrayal occurs in other texts: Joseph betrays his friend Obi by writing to his parents without Obi's knowledge to warn them that their son plans to marry an *osu* while Obi betrays the sturdy faith that Clara has in him. In *A Man of the People*, however, each character behaves in ways that reflect badly on them, motivated as they are by self-interest. Odili betrays the hospitality the Nangas offer by building on his newly found political confidence gained in their home to contest Chief Nanga's seat. Mr Nwege, the headmaster, dismisses him for his arrogance in holding himself above Nanga and above his post as schoolteacher: 'I see you have grown too big for your coat' (*MP* 102). Nanga himself issues a litany of charges against 'Odili the great' in order to rally the election crowd in his home village of Anata – even betrayal can be turned to political advantage (*MP* 139). And betrayal turns into a physical fight in the election-heady crowd: 'The roar of the crowd was now like a thick forest all around. By this time blows were falling as fast as rain on my head and body until something heavier than the rest seemed to split my skull. The last thing I remembered was seeing all the policemen turn round and walk quietly away' (*MP* 140). *A Man of the People* is filled with sexual and political betrayal, but this last example represents the turning away of a social service from one in need – until it becomes clear that the 'police' were disguised party thugs supporting Nanga. Gikandi asserts that Odili 'wants us to read the rise and fall of Nanga as an allegory of the promise and the betrayal of nationalism' and it is through Achebe's creation of a spikey first-person narrator/witness that he succeeds in commentating on the outlandish eccentricities of the political process in the 'new nation'.[11]

BEARING WITNESS

In 'The Role of the Writer in the New Nation', Achebe discusses the writer as witness and the temptation to idealize traditional societies that might make of him an untrustworthy witness. He uses an effective analogy to convey the way the past may be filtered through the writer's lens:

> I always think of light and glass. When white light hits glass one of two things can happen. Either you have an image which is faithful if somewhat unexciting or you have a glorious spectrum which though beautiful is really a distortion. Light from the past passes through a kind of glass to reach us. We can either look for the accurate but maybe unexciting image or we can look for the glorious technicolour.[12]

The witness-participant has long been a significant literary device for writers for whom national politics is a component of the fictional world they create, and bearing witness is one of the key impulses behind Achebe's fiction. In *A Man of the People* Odili is a technicolour witness who regales the reader with his version of events. Robert Holton's idea of the 'jarring witness' is of a character whose voice has traditionally been suppressed but, in novels that engage with the problems of historiography and truth-telling, comes to speak from the margins of dominant discourse.[13] An omniscient narrator provides commentary on Obi's thoughts but Odili is more confident than his literary predecessor and, while functioning as a witness, he is also the control in a literary experiment to uncover bribery and corruption. Odili is Achebe's only sustained foray into first-person narration as a literary form and structuring principle outside of the short-story form.

Odili's narrative is written in what he calls 'cold print'. It is a controlled narrative written with hindsight and posed as the 'master narrative' of events that led to the murder of Max and the coup that brought down a corrupt government. Of his meeting with Nanga in the first chapter he assures the reader, 'My memory is naturally good. That day was perfect. I don't know how it happened, but I can recall every word the Minister said on that occasion. I can repeat the entire speech he made' (*MP* 9). Odili maintains he is an effective and reliable witness and generic sentences like the one that opens the novel are an effective device through which to control the narrative: 'No one can deny that Chief the Honourable M. A. Nanga, M. P., was the most approachable politician in the country'.

77

While apparently lending authentication, they are more closely aligned with the corrosive corruption that the ironically titled *The Daily Machet* reports. Odili uses them to satirical effect throughout: 'As the whole world now knows . . .' and 'The events of the next four weeks or so have become so widely known in the world at large that there would be little point in my relating them in any detail here' (*MP* 140).

Odili struggles to make what is not coherent – the political twists and turns of a corrupt government – into a phased and comprehensive narrative. But Odili is hoisted by his own narratorial petard: he wishes to include everything so that when Elsie, the girlfriend he lost to Chief Nanga, enters the story he has difficulty in conveying her function in the tale aside from her function in his life:

> Where does one begin to write about her? The difficulty in writing this kind of story is that the writer is armed with all kinds of hindsight which he didn't have when the original events were happening. When he introduces a character like Elsie for instance, he already has at the back of his mind a total picture of her; her entrance, her act and her exit. . . . I shall try not to jump ahead of my story. (*MP* 23–4)

Such metafictional anxieties about presenting the 'total picture' capture the unreliability of a narrator stung by events: Elsie and Nanga's betrayal is one such event in a novel overloaded with incidents which challenge the authority he accords his testimony. Odili's words and thoughts betray their self-centred search for meaning on his own terms, casting himself as a hero who is saved from 'Nangaism' by his own political acumen and, finally, by the love of a good woman (Edna) and the moral force of the village (his father). But they are also the root of the conclusions he draws and, as Gikandi points out, the language others use is often dismissed as cliché in order to elevate the language forms Odili selects to convey his own elevated position in the narrative ('I became a hero in the eyes of the crowd' and 'What I had to accomplish became more than another squabble for political office; it rose suddenly to the heights of symbolic action, a shining, monumental gesture untainted by hopes of success or reward', *MP* 130). Odili is perfectly capable of flying upwards in lofty language and equally capable of condemning himself from his own mouth. He is one of Achebe's most engaging characters. His narration in all its irony is prototypical for the mixed narrative forms that Achebe experiments with in *Anthills of the Savannah*.

A Man of the People is a far more hard-hitting satire than *No Longer at Ease*: it marks the shift from colonial to postcolonial fiction in Achebe's oeuvre and from irony to satire, and even downright farce. For Ngugi it marks another change too, in which the novelist as teacher loses patience:

> What Achebe has done in *A Man of the People* is to make it impossible for other African writers to do other than address themselves directly to their audiences in Africa – not in a comforting spirit – and tell them that such problems are their concern. The teacher no longer stands apart to contemplate. He has moved with a whip among the pupils, flagellating himself as well as them. He is now the true man of the people.[14]

As one reads into Achebe's oeuvre, it becomes very apparent that his protagonists are progressively more acculturated. While Eguewe in *Arrow of God* assigns rituals to his sons to substantiate their ongoing connection to the clan and to forge continuity, Obi is given the space to chase a European lifestyle that is fast diminishing in the hope that his progression through the ranks of the civil service will glorify his clansmen. Obi's final disillusionment is that he is unable to find the equilibrium that will restore his self worth; caught in the nets of urban 'progress', he is unfit for the struggle between the Appolonian and the Dionysian within his character. Obi has moved from representing Umuofia's hope in the future to functioning as a warning for those who come after him to season their ambition with a heightened moral sense. The hedonistic and self-seeking urges Obi and Odili follow in dissolute cities like Lagos led them to kick against social responsibility and the value of rural community and home, issues that Achebe returns to in *Anthills of the Savannah*.

In *A Man of the People*, military intervention is the symbolic solution to the problem of a dissolute leadership represented by Chief Nanga. When a few days after the novel's publication a military coup took place, Achebe suddenly found himself in the eye of a storm. There were rumours that he had supported or even engineered the unsuccessful coup. Despite the fact that some twenty years pass before *Anthills of the Savannah*, it is clear that in the time that elapses between 1966 and 1987 Nigeria sinks into a morass of violence and corruption that Achebe can only begin to touch on in *A Man of the People*. Nigeria's polity has remained unstable but, as one writer-observer argues, 'Fear of the military is the beginning of political wisdom in Nigeria'.[15] Chief Nanga and Odili represent the height of Achebe's comedic sense and the basis for the political wisdom that is distilled in *Anthills of the Savannah*. When Achebe writes of seeking out 'one shining act of bold, selfless leadership, such as unambiguous refusal to be corrupt or tolerate corruption at the fountain of authority' (*TN* 17), he provides no example from life. In his fiction it is Obi who posits the possibility that an 'enlightened dictator' could lead the nation out of corruption. Achebe does not conceive of such a man in fictional terms and Nanga is the closest he gets to portraying the kind of charismatic performance that can seduce the people into believing in such a man. Bernth Lindfors calls Nanga 'one of the finest rogues in African fiction', but 'one needed to look into the very heart of the body politic to account for such a diseased member ... The society had to undergo a major political convulsion before such cynicism was transmuted into hope'.[16] This is the task Achebe sets himself in his final novel.

5

The Trouble with Nigeria:
Anthills of the Savannah

We carry in our worlds that flourish
Our worlds that have failed . . .

> (Christopher Okigbo,
> 'Lament of the Silent Sisters', 1963)

That is Africa your Africa
That grows again patiently obstinately
And its fruit gradually acquire
The bitter taste of liberty.

> (David Diop, 'Africa', 1956)

Our country is an *abiku* country. Like the spirit-child, it
keeps coming and going. One day it will decide to remain.
It will become strong.

> (Ben Okri, *The Famished Road*, 1991)

In 1983 Achebe published a little book of around sixty pages
that he described as a 'hazardous enterprise' even though he
allows that 'Whenever two Nigerians meet, their conversation
will sooner or later slide into a litany of our national defi-
ciencies' (*TN* 2). The country's troubles have become aphoris-
tic. In *The Trouble with Nigeria*, Achebe lucidly spells out that
he believes their root cause is the failure of leadership: coups
and assassinations, violence and corruption, election riots and
civil war have characterized the country's history post-Independence. By December of its year of publication, yet another
political coup had taken place. In the role of novelist Achebe
finds creative ways in which to reveal the corrupt scourge of
the new nation, as in *A Man of the People* through the rise of
profligate Chief Nanga. In this novel, the index of patriotism is

made achingly clear: in postcolonial Nigeria, ministers are *de facto* spokesmen for ethnic interests, notably for their own ethnic group's access to the 'national cake'. That is, until their individual accumulation of wealth and privilege supersedes all political considerations, precipitating the nation into moral bankruptcy. In *The Trouble with Nigeria*, Achebe is scathing about Nigerians 'falling prey' to ethnic nationalisms and about the 'bankrupt state' of leadership from within his own ethnic group. Despite a history of Igbo republicanism, he observes 'mushroom kingships': 'From having no kings in their recent past the Igbo swung round to set an all-time record of four hundred "kings" in Imo and four hundred in Anambra! And most of them are traders in their stall by day and monarchs at night . . .' (*TN* 48).

In *A Man of the People*, Odili believes he penetrates 'man's basic nature' through natural metaphors: 'The trouble with our new nation . . . was . . . We had all been in the rain together until yesterday. Then a handful of us – the smart and the lucky and hardly ever the best – had scrambled for the one shelter our former rulers left, and had taken it over and barricaded themselves in' (*MP* 37). Although Achebe casts these as a self-important young man's 'elevated thoughts', the idea of the government sheltering in a storm receives sustained ironic consideration in *Anthills of the Savannah*. After the first phase of national 'struggle', Odili describes the second, which requires 'that all argument should cease and the whole people speak with one voice and that any more dissent and argument outside the door of the shelter would subvert and bring down the whole house' (*MP* 37). Later in *Anthills of the Savannah*, an 'unseasonal tropical storm' in the month of August heralds the events that will bring yet another corrupt and incompetent leader to the eve of another coup. Although politically Achebe always occupies the middle ground, he would seem to agree with Marxist historian Eric Hobsbawm who traces such catastrophes back to the destruction of a sense of public past, 'or rather the social mechanisms that link one's contemporary experience to that of earlier generations'. For Hobsbawm, the risk is that young people will grow up in 'a sort of permanent present lacking any organic relation to the public past'.[1] This form of regret floats through *Anthills of the Savannah*.

In fact, only a year after Achebe published *The Trouble with Nigeria*, General Buhari declared that there was really little point in the country celebrating the twenty-fourth anniversary of its Independence from Britain because the new nation's history was a source of shame rather than celebration. The twenty-fifth anniversary, in 1985, was similarly subdued, while inside the shelter of government house corruption simmered to boiling point. Over the first twenty-five years of self-rule that pass before Achebe begins writing *Anthills of the Savannah*, Nigeria suffered eight governments under different elected and military leaders. The first coup d'état in 1966 was known as the majors' coup and it has remained a potent symbol of national unrest because many of the same majors who challenged the first independent government (Buhari and Babangida, for example) were to become corrupt rulers themselves following subsequent coups.

The nationalist rhetoric of Independence in the 1960s did not translate into concrete social programmes. As late as 1981, the federal government took out a series of advertisements in the British press to promote Nigerian democracy and the new federal capital city, Abuja instead of Lagos.[2] Clearly, such promotional advertisements had limited success in convincing either a sceptical former colonizer or many Nigerians that the new nation could be a model of democratic strength in Africa. As long ago as 1964, Ernest Gellner argued that, far from signalling the awakening of a nation to self-conscious government, nationalism 'invents nations where they do not exist'. In similar fashion, Benedict Anderson's classic study *Imagined Communities* (1983), in which community is the organizing trope of nation, adjudges that anything larger than a 'primordial village' can no longer realistically call itself a community (national or otherwise). The national 'community' becomes imagined rather than real.[3] In a *Guardian* special report on Nigeria conducted in 1985, Ad' Obe Obe discusses the 'shaky national rationale' whereby 'each new regime promises to be what the last one was not'. In the same newspaper, David Pallister argues that the yardsticks that ordinary people use to judge a regime tend to be 'the price of a bag of rice, a packet of detergent and a tin of nursing milk'. Such items remained inflated whichever regime held the reins of power.[4]

In the late 1970s, national leader Olusegun Obasanjo had vowed that Nigeria would become one of the ten leading nations in the world by the end of the twentieth century. Achebe argues that Obasanjo's particular fantasy is an illustration of a 'cargo cult mentality' whereby underdeveloped countries believe progressive change will take place 'without any exertion whatsoever on their part' (*TN* 9). Ironically, Obasanjo's second term of office coincided with the end of the century and he is yet to fulfil his own stated hopes. In fact, in the two years before Obasanjo took office in 1998, Soni Abacha had led 'peace-keeping' forces in Liberia during its civil war – but Nigerian troops looted Monrovia when the city was destroyed in 1996. Nigeria also resolved to help Sierra Leone down the rocky road to free democratic elections in 1997, even though its own government was criticized for not facing problems at home.

Tellingly, Achebe begins his polemical study of the national situation not with Obasanjo but with Mohammed Murtala. Murtala ruled once, and for only six months, in 1975, before being murdered during a botched coup, but he came to personify the dwindling hopes of many ordinary Nigerians – across ethnic groups – for solid leadership and committed action in a nation bereft of political straight-talking. General Murtala outlined the policy guidelines for the Nigerian Constitution as part of a process in which the military would relinquish power to a federal, elected government. This transfer of power took place in 1979, under the leadership of Obasanjo. The country then became the world's fourth largest democracy under President Alhaji Shehu Shagari (1979–83). He was an unusual figure in the history of Nigerian politics for the sheer fact that he had been a member of a series of different governments for a total of twenty-one years (1958–79), largely untouched by coups and counter-coups. Nevertheless, by 1983 Achebe declares with undisguised dismay that Nigeria is, indeed, 'one of the most corrupt, insensitive, inefficient places under the sun . . . dirty, callous, noisy, ostentatious, dishonest and vulgar' (*TN* 9) and Wole Soyinka, looking back on Shagari's term in office from the vantage point of 1993, declares him 'a disaster': 'not even his greatest admirers would deny that he was a disaster for the nation in terms of policy decisions implementation. His reign was a zero, a minus'.[5] In 1993, Nigerian elections were annulled by the Babangida regime and rumours abounded that their political opposition, in the person of Chief Abiola, had been placed under house arrest. Abiola's wife was later assassinated. The leadership of the modern nation was flawed from its inception with rigged elections, money for votes, and material excesses dominating international headlines. Over the years the issue of leadership has congealed into ethnic enclaves that have promoted the kind of sectionalism that militates against national and political unity. Though commentators have seen a confederacy or devolution as a possible solution to 'the Nigerian problem' of militarized ethnic nationalism, so far any alternative to the Federal Republic of Nigeria has received scant recognition and the 'trouble' with Nigeria remains a problem with which writers and political commentators contend.

Achebe has always been a political writer but not in a programmatic way. He combines the roles of teacher and social commentator, and takes care to differentiate the passionate declarative essays from the novels, as discussed in chapter 1. Achebe has contributed much more to an exposé of the manipulation of state power by the military than is initially apparent to those who continue to characterize him by his early work: first in *A Man of the People* and later, more discursively, in *Anthills of the Savannah*. The former ended with a coup and the latter begins after the leaders of a coup have become firmly ensconced as government. The soldiers-turned-politicians have become more violent and corrupt than those they sought to correct. By the end of *Anthills of the Savannah* there is another coup in the roller-coaster ride that is the political history of 'Kangan', a fictional West African state. The novel begins *in medias res*, in the midst of a political argument that immediately conveys to the reader that the machinery of corrupt government has been cranking away for some time. In the very first chapter, Achebe takes the reader straight from a Cabinet meeting to gruesome scenes of crowds enjoying a public execution. He makes pointed references to the shooting of striking rail workers and demonstrating students as well as the banning of unions. Secret police, known ironically as the 'State Research Council', silence dissent at all levels: 'There were unconfirmed rumours of unrest, secret trials and executions in the barracks' (*AS* 14). Their boss, Colonel Johnson Ossai, is compared to Idi Amin on more than one occasion and when he disappears late in the novel few are concerned.

The Head of State, 'His Excellency' Sam, is a Sandhurst-trained military officer who takes power through one military coup, only to lose his presidency in another. Achebe imagines Sam as the archetypal ruler who alienates himself from those he rules. He has ostensibly mastered each phase of the nation's belaboured political progress: 'the first African Second Lieutenant in the Army; ADC to the Governor General; Royal Equerry during the Queen's visit; Officer Commanding at Independence; Colonel at the time of the coup; General and His Excellency, the Head of State' (*AS* 67). His oldest friends are Chris Oriko, Commissioner for Information, and Ikem Osodi, editor of the *National Gazette*, but Sam is fast losing sight of friendship and relations are strained by his autocratic control. The 'trouble with Nigeria' is told from Chris's and Ikem's points of view along with that of Beatrice Okoh, Chris's girlfriend and a Senior Secretary in the Ministry of Finance. One way in which this novel differs from previous ones is that the story fails to cohere. Achebe does raise the problem of coherence in earlier novels, via the circumlocutory tale of Obi's downfall and via the first-person narration of *A Man of the People*. In that novel Odili searches for a voice and a form in which to communicate with truth and integrity a political story in which he is himself a biased participant. Almost twenty years later, however, Ikem, Chris and Beatrice, overwhelmed by events, discover they have no personal-historical memory of a time *before* political corruption took hold to aid them in the task of explaining the present. They have lost their connection to the tales and proverbs that fortified previous generations and which provided them with a system of values. Geographically they are also marooned in a city in which they have become unsafe. Whereas Odili finds his way back to his home village, Abazon where Ikem and Beatrice were born is a fragile symbol. The political fight must be won first in the metropolis at the seat of corruption and in the crucible of violence. For example, when Chris attempts to tender his resignation to Sam late in the novel, he is met with laughter: 'Where do you think you are? Westminster or Washington DC? Come on! This is a military government in a backward West African State' (*AS* 144).

The situation that the narrators bear witness to spirals out of control. When he speaks publicly against Sam, Ikem is murdered; Chris goes into hiding and is later killed by chance in a violent encounter in which he saves a young woman from being raped by a drunken officer of the law. Their deaths echo other deaths, like the murder of Max in *A Man of the People* which helps to light 'the tinder of discontent in the land' (*MP* 143). They may also recall actual murders, like that of Dele Giwa, the editor of the magazine *Newswatch*, killed by a parcel bomb in October of 1986. Sam is killed when his government topples. Beatrice and Elewa, Ikem's girlfriend and the mother of his soon-to-be-born child, are left to pick up the pieces and to go on. The final chapter, or epilogue, sees them beginning to do precisely that in the company of a disparate group of like-minded friends. Out of the period of mourning that follows the murders, and in a spirit of recovery, they begin to discuss reform with Beatrice as 'a captain whose leadership was sharpened more and more by sensitivity to the peculiar needs of her company' (*AS* 229). Achebe imagines a small community with a woman at its centre. Beatrice is named for the silent inspirational muse at the heart of European literature, but here she is reworked as the voice of reason in the inferno of African politics.

SEASON OF ANOMY: CIVIL WAR

One reading of *Anthills of the Savannah* would be to see it as Achebe's deferred response to civil war as well as the ensuing governmental corruption that led him to write the pamphlet *The Trouble with Nigeria*. In the 1960s, Biafra was one of the most emotionally resonant causes in a decade of civil rights struggles around the world. Images the public now associates with Ethiopia and Rwanda courtesy of the Live Aid concert in 1984 and fundraisers since were first associated with Biafra. The world was shocked by television images of emaciated children with bloated stomachs starving on the wrong side of

87

a government blockade intended to prevent the secession of Eastern Nigeria from the rest of the body politic. Igbos in Eastern Nigeria founded the Republic of Biafra in 1967. Following the assassination of Prime Minister Balewa in the 1966 coup led by an Igbo, General Johnson Ironsi, there were riots protesting Ironsi's new regime in which thousands of Igbos living in the northern region of Nigeria were killed. Inter-ethnic enmity had been superimposed on the colonial template for government. Ironsi was himself deposed in July of 1967 in another coup in which General Yakubu Gowon took control, but civil war raged on, resulting in the loss of around two million lives. Chinua Achebe threw in his lot with Biafra as a diplomat, spokesman and fundraiser. Britain was heavily involved in the arming of Gowon's government in order to protect its trading interests. The majority of Nigeria's oil resources were located in Biafra, the eastern and predominantly Igbo region, and the blockade disallowed even (partly government-owned) Shell-BP oil from being exported. It was clear that Biafra would fall, but the Biafrans held out against internal and external pressures for three defiant years until 1970. Achebe goes some way towards expressing the stages of fading resistance in a short story about the ravages of war: 'Death and starvation having long chased out the headiness of the early days, now left in some places blank resignation, in others a rock-like, even suicidal defiance' (GW 106).

Wole Soyinka, imprisoned for denouncing the war (he was even rumoured to have been smuggling arms to Biafra) and the 'genocide-consolidated dictatorship' of Gowon's army, stated that the effects of war 'must shatter the foundations of thought and re-create'.[6] Nigerian writers gathered themselves to respond to the war and its aftermath and Soyinka's expression 'season of anomy', the title of his 1973 novel, succeeded in capturing the dispirited nation after the war. Achebe, having abandoned a novel for its irrelevancy at the beginning of the war, initially responded through poetry – 'Christmas in Biafra (1969)', 'After a War' and 'Public Execution in Pictures' in Beware, Soul Brother (1971) – and in the form of short stories like 'Girls at War' and 'Civil Peace'. The short stories typically focus on a single relationship or incident in order to convey a tranche, or cross-section, of life during the

war. In 'Girls at War' it is the relationship between Reginald
Nwankwo, Minister of Justice, and a young woman called
Gladys whose paths cross three times at different stages of the
war. The stories also contain passages in which one feels the
author is drawn closest to his narrator, reflecting on life behind
the blockade outside the action of the story itself:

> It was a tight, blockaded and desperate world. None the less a
> world – with some goodness and some badness and plenty of
> heroism which, however, happened most times far, far below the
> eye-level of the people in this story – in out-of-the-way refugee
> camps, in the damp tatters, in the hungry and bare-handed
> courage of the first line of fire. (GW 106)

Many writers deferred their 'war stories': Cyprian Ekwensi's
Survive the Peace came out in 1976 and Elechi Amadi's
Estrangement wasn't published until 1986. Amadi depicts Port
Harcourt two years after the end of the war with refugees
scrambling through detritus and blown-out buildings earmarked by the government and foreign construction companies:
'bombed buildings grinned like huge skulls. ... lunatics and
vagrants could be seen, moving inside them like maggots
finishing off the last chunks of flesh in the decaying skulls ...
a few restored buildings bore large signs of this ministry or
that. ... Foreign firms were particularly active'.[7] Younger
writers found that, long after the fall of Biafra, the civil war
remained a pressing subject for fiction. Ben Okri returns to the
war, as does Buchi Emecheta in *Destination Biafra* (1982). In the
aftermath of war, Achebe warned that Nigeria should not
pretend that slogans are the same as truths (*MYCD* xiii). One
imagines he had in mind Gowon's slogan for waging civil war
against Eastern Nigeria, 'To keep Nigeria one is a task that
must be done'. Slogans have been deployed at the most
strained moments in Nigeria's recent history and Gowon
coined another strategic slogan on defeating Biafra, 'No victor,
no vanquished' – the errant Biafrans could become Nigerians
again, once safely back in the national fold. Achebe's hatred of
slogans and of hackneyed phrasing is clear from *No Longer at
Ease*, where Obi substitutes glib quotation for concrete engagement. And in *A Man of the People* Odili learns to replace empty
spectacle (burning effigies in the Students' Union) and rhetoric

with commitment: at the end of the novel he is planning to found a school in his village. The shift from rhetoric to reform receives its most discursive treatment in his fifth novel, *Anthills of the Savannah*. The characters left alive at the end are 'like stragglers from a massacred army' (*AS* 217), an incredibly powerful image of war that recalls the poetry in *Beware Soul Brother*. The civil war comprises the sediment at the bottom of a heady mix in a novel that is richly layered and heavily politicized.

FICTION AND REFORM

In *The Trouble with Nigeria* Achebe addresses himself to the ruling elite on the eve of a scandalously corrupt election in 1983. Preceding the publication of *Anthills of the Savannah* in 1987, the nation was ruled by General Ibrahim Babangida, more generally known as 'the evil genius', who gave Mercedes cars to visiting national leaders and reputedly siphoned off around 12 billion US dollars from the nation's oil reserves. Nigerian politics has never been less than dramatic, peppered with scandals of a fiscal and sexual nature (Babangida's successor, Abacha, was reputed to have died while having sex with two prostitutes). After the collapse of Abacha's Nigeria it was suggested that a tribunal with a similar remit to South Africa's Truth and Reconciliation Committee might be set up to negotiate future harmony alongside national recovery. Literature sometimes contributes to the kind of political and social work that governments fail to implement. Writers like Achebe and Soyinka graft stories on to the nation and serve to accent issues that must be addressed in order to begin to foster national reconciliation. Among the tensions that influence Achebe's 1987 novel are the long-term impact of civil war on a disenchanted society and feminist claims to equality in a nation led by patriarchal soldiers-turned-politicians.

In a brave and ironic novel, Achebe brings together many of 'the broken pieces of this tragic history' (*AS* 82) into a mosaic, to borrow a phrase he attributes to Beatrice. He historicizes the pressures on Nigeria in the 1980s only partially disguised as the country of Kangan, so that the situation he describes may also echo other African national experiences. Kangan is squeezing the Abazonians, for whom drought is life-threatening, but the subject is of little or no concern to the country's leaders at its metropolitan centre ('Abazon . . . you know, the drought place', *AS* 57). The correlations with Biafra's secession and Achebe's polemical position in *The Trouble with Nigeria* are clear. National leadership fails to embody diverse communities and exploits ethnic and regional tensions. The Abazonian spokesmen in the novel are the first to approach the model of democracy that Achebe has come to espouse. In precolonial Igboland as depicted in earlier novels, for all the faults and tensions that punctuate tribal living, the principles of communal living remain paramount. Such ideals have been lost and Achebe's young people, seduced by the excesses of bourgeois materialism that they discover in urban centres like Bassa (Lagos in *No Longer at Ease* and Bori in *A Man of the People*), find their sense of self dissolving and any moral force dissipating.

Achebe works out some of his stated concerns in *The Trouble with Nigeria* but shifts more openly to encompass a much broader power base. In *Anthills of the Savannah* Achebe casts his net wider than usual to gather in a host of preoccupations via a gallery of characters: a noxious dictator with armed police and, at his fingertips, ministers and lackeys, students, taxi drivers, and market traders. This is not to say that the cast of characters is larger than in previous novels (one critic has counted fifty-seven characters in *Things Fall Apart*[8]). But as the African American writer Ralph Ellison pointed out, since democracy requires articulate people, novelists should be engaged in the creation of conscious, articulate characters.[9] And Achebe opens up the range in this final novel beyond the intellectual elite at its centre. The success of *Anthills of the Savannah* rests on its ability to be inclusive in its portrayal of politics, citizenship and civic responsibility; its espousal of democratic principles is set against the kleptocracies that have characterized Nigerian politics since the 1960s. The novel's political effects are poignantly felt in the portrayal of Abazon and its representatives, decent and modulated elders who come to Kangan's capital city Bassa only to be spurned by Sam. While Abazon can not be simplistically equated with the

Republic of Biafra, the dismissal of the group as 'ignorant believers in rainmakers' (AS 4) and the description of their illegal imprisonment for marching to the palace without a permit is shot through with stinging anger. The seeds of hope the novel sows are largely de-tribalized, however: Beatrice, Chris and Ikem privilege nation over state and each becomes progressively more open and able to communicate across ethnic divisions. The novel is set against the tribalistic disaffection that resulted in civil war.

One of Achebe's closest friends, the poet Christopher Okigbo died defending Nsukka during the civil war. Achebe admired him as a poet who, he said, 'conjured up for us an amazing, haunting poetic firmament of a world and violent beauty' (MYCD 28). Okigbo ghosts Anthills of the Savannah; traces of his character can be found in both Ikem and Chris. Chris Oriko dies with a young student, Emmanuel, crying helplessly at his side, 'Please sir, don't go' (AS 216). They are simple words that echo the essay 'Don't Let Him Die: A Tribute to Christopher Okigbo' (1978) in which Achebe remembers his own young son devastated by news of Okigbo's death screaming 'Daddy, don't let him die' (HI 79). Ikem Osodi has something of Okigbo's poetic talent; he thinks in 'strong, even exaggerated images' (AS 140). His apocalyptic 'Hymn to the Sun' (AS 30) echoes Okigbo's own Sunbird, killed in 'Fragments out of the Deluge', but who sings after death of Guernica (a painting of war by Picasso) 'on whose canvas of blood / The slits of his tongue / cling to glue . . . / & the cancelling out is complete'.[10] It is in Ikem's poetry that Achebe's title metaphor finds its place in the novel: 'anthills surviving to tell the new grass of the savannah about last year's brush fires' (AS 31). In the conflation of the residual and the new, Achebe echoes two of Okigbo's most famous lines:

> We carry in our worlds that flourish
> Our worlds that have failed . . .[11]

While it is not an idealistic novel, Chris knows when he sees the anthills in the scrubland of Abazon he has chosen as 'sanctuary' after Ikem's death that 'the searing accuracy of the poet's eye was primed not on fantasy but fact' (AS 209). Most critics who read Anthills of the Savannah contend that hope for the redemption of Africa is contained in such images. Indeed, Achebe has spoken of the possibility of a 'new dispensation' at the end of the novel, echoing T. S. Eliot's poetry as borrowed in *No Longer at Ease* and bringing the novelist's concerns full circle.[12] The novel offers a qualified hope that is somewhat offset by the narrative strategies used to convey it.

Anthills of the Savannah is the most vertiginous of Achebe's fictions. He combines three perspectives with that of an omniscient narrator, and complicates the structure with flash-backs and densely poetic intertexts like the 'Hymn to the Sun' and David Diop's poem 'Africa'. In the intervening period between *A Man of the People* and *Anthills of the Savannah* fictional culture changed. Achebe had been working on a fifth novel that his biographer tells us was intended to synthesize the major themes raised by the earlier novels. But he abandoned the novel as fragments. Forms of realism give way to postmodernist strategies, despite the references to moments in Africa's history that anchor the novel, and the overall effect is more disorienting and fragmented than previous fictions. Of the novel's multiple narrators, Chris and Ikem are dead, their testimony echoing beyond the situation they describe and beyond their own individual fates, and Beatrice though grounded is also quite mystical, a reincarnation of a village priestess 'who will prophesy when her divinity rules' (*AS* 105). Sam does not speak or appear, except through reported speech. On the very first page of the novel, Chris, in his role as Commissioner for Information, admonishes 'His Excellency' that he should make a formal visit to Abazon. His refusal and dismissal of his adviser ('But me no buts, Mr Oriko!') prompts Chris to reply testily – only to be met with silence. Sam uses silence, 'making the silence itself grow rapidly into its own kind of contest, like the eyewink duel of children' (*AS* 1). In a polyvocal novel in which speech-making figures so prominent-ly, Sam's silence signals the mendacity associated with political leadership. Sam strives to silence the Abazonians' dissent – even though it is couched in the homiletic elders' expressions of folkloric wisdom – by systematically starving them into submission. He ensures that the independent voice of the press, in the person of Ikem, is compromised. For the auto-cratic Sam, the press is merely a tool through which he may disseminate his command. Sam's own silence in the text is an ironic comment on the kind of strawman that can stand at the centre of Nigerian politics and on the stage-management of his government.

Public speeches to large audiences find a place in each of Achebe's works. Achebe critiques the empty speeches made by those who declaim solely in order to hear their own voices or to celebrate their own position (Nwaka, on occasion, in *Arrow of God* and Chief Nanga in *A Man of the People*). In *Anthills of the Savannah*, Emmanuel feels his life transformed listening to Ikem: 'The ideas in one lecture by Ikem changed my entire life from a parrot to a man' (*AS* 223). Small-group debates ignite engaged political conversation in which nationhood becomes the bread-and-butter topic of all thinking citizens. But the exchanges that take place between intellectuals in the novel heighten the dilemma of how to *interpret* their situation. Chris longs to find the moment when things fell apart, but fails, and Ikem distils his own epistemological crisis in his poetry. Achebe described Christopher Okigbo's poetry as 'an anguished journey back from alienation to resumption of ritual and priestly functions' (*MYCD* 28) and it is the 'journey back' to a community from which he has been severed that animates Ikem in the days and hours prior to his death. In the lecture he delivers at the university, Ikem cites the story he learned from the Abazonian elder imprisoned by Sam to demonstrate that storytellers threaten a corrupt status quo. The narrator forges a link back to tradition through Ikem's speech and his poetry and through the story of Idemili, Beatrice's avatar who is sent to bear witness. Beatrice's dreams in which she becomes Nwanyibuife and emerges a village priestess, Chielo, whose story was repressed throughout Beatrice's Christian upbringing, configure an additional layer in the narrative. As Simon Gikandi suggests, the novel is a search for an African hermeneutics and each intellectual tries to 'find a voice to articulate the desires and yearnings, even the idealism, that motivated them at an earlier stage in the decolonization process'.[13]

At one level the novel is a love story, but Achebe pulls back to transfer the feelings Beatrice devoted to Chris into hopes for national reform. Romantic relationships figure in both *No*

Longer at Ease and *A Man of the People*, but Obi squanders the possibility of love and happiness. He begins by being strongly attracted to Clara at a dance in England and their meeting again aboard ship seals their relationship but he becomes increasingly self-involved until he begins to rely on Clara financially instead of emotionally. Obi's parents' disapproval of her loosens what hold she retains on his affections, despite her pregnancy. She turns away, her self-preservation stronger than his lack of interest. Odili is a sensual man who has sex often but scant sense of romantic fulfilment until the very final pages when Achebe salvages his relationship with Edna. Only in *Anthills of the Savannah* is there a strong sense of emotional involvement between men and women behaving as equals. The scene in which Chris and Beatrice make love is the most sensual and sensuous of Achebe's oeuvre. However, he chooses a platonic model on which to base his quiet, residual hopes for the new nation.

A NATIONAL 'FAMILY'

In *No Longer at Ease* there is a rare scene in which Obi, Clara and an Englishman, John Macmillan, become sudden friends. They are easy in each other's company aboard the ship that takes them from England to Nigeria in the dog days of British rule. They share food, wine and laughter and after an evening's jaunt on shore return to the ship, 'Macmillan holding Clara's right hand and Obi her left' (*NLE* 25). Importantly, the ship, like many others deployed in literature, is isolated, floating off society's limits. The haven the group finds there is transient and the Nigerians never meet the Englishman again. Achebe stretches beyond the idea of sanctuary in *Anthills of the Savannah* to test other more viable models for cross-cultural national progress. The brotherhood between Sam, Ikem and Chris is a model on which the nation has foundered; a nepotistic model of government that ends with three friends estranged and then murdered, the one having first betrayed the other two. In *The Trouble with Nigeria*, Achebe deploys the national anthem (composed by an Englishwoman) to make a bitter reference to Nigerians 'standing or sprawling on a soil soaked in fratricidal blood'. First sung in 1960 to memorialize Independence, its words have a bitter resonance: 'Though tribe and tongue may differ / In brotherhood we stand'. Sam, Chris and Ikem share a history and the crime that Sam commits in hunting down the friends who challenged his dictatorship may therefore be read as a symbolic fratricide. His sycophantic Attorney General encourages Sam in paranoid speculation about Chris: 'I don't think Chris is one hundred percent behind you. . . . you were after all classmates at Lord Lugard College. . . . He cannot understand how this same boy with whom he played all the boyish pranks, how he can today become this nation's Man of Destiny. You know, Your Excellency it was the same trouble Jesus had to face with his people' (*AS* 23).

Even intellectual dissent is construed as traitorous. In Ikem's fiery speech to the students, he quotes a 'fantastic' proverb that his ancestors used to distinguish between direct and indirect causes: 'If you want to get at the root of murder . . . you have to look for the blacksmith who made the machete' (*AS* 159). The audience laughs. However, the reader returns to the proverb with the benefit of hindsight when only a few pages later Ikem is shot while in police custody. A headline in the *National Gazette* cites his advocating of 'regicide'; Ikem is the wordsmith who makes the words that kill a 'king'. Those words are the indirect cause of his own death, although it is Sam's Security Forces who commit the deed and try to hide it: 'One of the ifs of recent Kangan history is what the fate of Ikem might have been had he backed out of that speaking engagement at the university' (*AS* 162). Sam is the blacksmith who made the symbolic machete with which he armed a corrupt police force, and the proverb returns us to *Things Fall Apart* and Okonkwo's striking down of the colonial messenger with a machete. Okonkwo felt he was acting honourably, unlike Sam. In this way Sam's habit of referring to his national responsibilities idiomatically as preparing for his funeral ('When it is your funeral you jolly well must think of everything') is made even more ironic. The 'trinity who thought they owned Kangan' (or Igbo, Hausa-Fulani and Yoruba if one stretches the metaphor) have fallen like so many 'green bottles'(*AS* 191). Chris comes to this realization in death and a fragment of a British popular song is the last ironic phrase on his lips. 'The last green . . . [bottle]' is a nod to Beatrice who foresaw the end of their triptych of power ('the story of Kangan is the story of the three of you') in favour of a broad-based coalition of political voices.

Ikem comes to the realization that any elite risks becoming alienated from 'the vital inner links with the poor and the dispossessed of this country, with the bruised heart that throbs painfully at the core of the nation's being' (AS 141). The scene in which two taxi drivers seek out the *oga* Ikem is a case in point. Their visit (primarily to apologize for having pursued an argument in a traffic jam) exhilarates him because of the 'rare human contact across station and class'. The taxi drivers, who have 'every cause to feel hatred' for the privileged few, come instead 'with friendship, acting out spontaneously and without self-righteousness what their betters preach so often but so seldom practise' (AS 136). The chapter in which Ikem and the taxi drivers converse is entitled 'Impetuous Son' and Ikem realizes that the taxi drivers deliver him a couple of verbal 'body-blows': they cannot entirely contain their resentment for the 'Mercedes-Benz-driving, private-jet-flying, luxury-yacht-cruising oppressor' (AS 138). However, as they speak, a light is shone in the vacuous darkness that is the yawning gap between rich and poor sons in postcolonial Nigeria. Trust is established and, when Chris's life is in danger, one of the taxi drivers is instrumental in helping him evade the security forces.

The national model on which the novel closes comprises elements of other potential models of reconciliation. It involves a naming ceremony: Ikem and Elewa's child, born after her father's death, is an unsurprising motif for hope in future generations. But the ceremony itself reorients a traditional ceremony into a modern rite of passage. It crosses classes, genders, generations and religious differences and it involves civilians and the military. It is intriguing that Achebe recuperates the military presence but it requires some tricky footwork for the plot. Captain Abdul Medani, who first met Beatrice when instructed to search her house for the fugitive Chris, becomes the anonymous caller she trusts to tell her when his hiding places should be changed. He undermines the regime's success from within because he has a good heart. It is he who returns with news of Chris's death and, when Beatrice refuses

97

to attend the state funeral that the incoming military Head of State organizes for Chris, he who is charged with keeping her under surveillance. Instead, he stays around in support and in trust (when old folk talk in a language he does not understand, Emmanuel translates and Abdul nods his head in agreement more vociferously than anyone else). Emmanuel's distrust of him is overcome and a cross-ethnic bond begins between the two men who debate the nation's future with animation but without rancour. The final chapter comprises one of the most didactic scenes of Achebe's fiction. He does not entirely forgo his usual irony but the central aphorism, 'This world belongs to the people of the world not to a little caucus, no matter how talented' (*AS* 232), is the novel's summation. Rather than coming together based on affinity or love or familial responsibility, the tired 'stragglers from a massacred army' form 'a defensive pact' and this between 'a small band of near-strangers' is to 'prove stronger than kindred or mere friendship' (*AS* 217–18). This scene is the closest Achebe has come in fiction to lobbying for a cross-ethnic political pact.

At the end of *The Trouble with Nigeria*, Achebe detected a 'powerful impulse' in Nigeria's consciousness 'towards a politics of peace and fair play', held in check by 'the dead grip of patriarchs' in what he sees as 'an obsolete dispensation' (*TN* 61). As C. L. Innes has pointed out, in *No Longer at Ease* it is the male characters' attitudes to the women in their lives that point the reader towards understanding not only individual men but also the government's dismissal of its electorate.[14] And, in *A Man of the People*, he shows how women are co-opted for corruption, 'breast-feeding the ballot' by concealing votes in their brassieres and smuggling them into polling booths (*MP* 143) or, more generally, simply fail to identify with the closed political system. Edna's mother is scathing when told that Odili will stand for election against Nanga: 'What is my share in that? They are both white men's people. And they know what is what between themselves. What do we know?' (*MP* 106). It is in *Anthills of the Savannah* that Achebe begins to *revise* his images of women, and the novel serves as Achebe's first tentative experiment with a model for national politics in which women might play not only a symbolic but also a political role.

REPRESENTING WOMEN

A story that Flora Nwapa has told involves Chinua Achebe as the Commissioning Editor for the Heinemann African Writers Series, accepting the manuscript of her first novel with an observation about its opening, in which a young woman steals away from home to live with the man she loves. Achebe was reputedly unconvinced that such a scene was credible in Igbo society, especially in a novel set in the 1940s. Nwapa explained that Oguta, her own village, was very different from the one in which Achebe grew up, in that independent women were often economically quite powerful and sexually confident. The novel, *Efuru*, was published in 1966 making Nwapa the first black African woman to publish a novel. Her anecdote is indicative of two things. On the one hand, it expresses the tension between traditional and modern ideas that character-izes Nigerian literature and the way that women become symbolic carriers of such ideas. But it also demonstrates something of the eclecticism of Igbo peoples in Nigeria and, by extension, of the literature that they produce. Achebe, who had no established literary tradition on which to draw when he began to write, learned something from the encounter.

Achebe, a novelist situated, as this study shows, on the cusp of traditional and modern Africa, has occasionally been criticized by feminist critics for his portrayals of women characters. For some readers it may seem anachronistic that a writer should be castigated for failing to slice through gender inequities in the 1950s and early 1960s when most male writers, whichever literary tradition they wrote within, were limited in the attention they paid to issues of gender. However, Achebe is largely absent from important essay collections in which representations of African women are critiqued[15] be-cause he does not idealize women and motherhood in excess of the Igbo traditions he re-imagines. Nor does he deploy women characters as symbols of the nation in the tradition of Negritude (Camara Laye's *The African Child* is a far clearer example). In fact, he parodies Leopold Senghor, the poet of Negritude in Max's ode to the 'Earth Mother' in *A Man of the People*. In *Things Fall Apart* women *are* wives and mothers ('Mother is Supreme'), but Achebe begins to deconstruct such images even within the 'traditional' novels. For example, Ezinma the 'changeling' daughter is her father's pride and joy and while he surreptitiously wishes she had been born a boy, the reader is aware that his judgement is skewed by his failure to reconcile himself to the 'feminine' principles that other Umuofians cherish. Okonkwo's ideal of 'masculine' endeavour is limited by his lack of understanding of women's worth: he designates cassava and beans 'women's crops' and mistakes his father's gentleness for femininity (see chapter 3). When Okonkwo expresses sentimental attachment to a person or a tradition, he chides himself for lapsing into 'womanly' traits. Taunting a man with behaving like *agbala* is the first insult that comes to Okonkwo's mind. His anger at his son's conversion to Christianity even prompts him to dismiss Nwoye as 'effeminate': 'How could he have begotten a woman for a son? (*TFA* 134). In a broader sense he is dismissive of 'women's stories' and he is contemptuously short with those who he feels lack his industry or his willingness to fight – or who simply dare to contradict him. When a clansman contradicts him during a meeting at which many are gathered, Okonkwo turns on the man, 'This meeting is for men'. All present side against Okonkwo and he is persuaded to apologize. On another occasion, Ekwefi, Okonkwo's second wife and the mother of Ezinma, demonstrates what fearlessness is when she braves the darkness and the night spirits to safeguard her daughter. As Ato Quayson has argued, it is possible to read the story of Ekwefi's challenging of a priestess, Chielo, and the male god she serves, Agbala, as 'subverting the patriarchal discourse of the text'.[16] Okonkwo follows at a safe distance, perhaps failing to completely master his fears even for his favourite child Ezinma.

The narrator undermines Okonkwo on a number of occasions in *Things Fall Apart*, intimating that it is foolish to deride others or to underestimate women's social roles or their individual significance. But in any case, Okonkwo is hardly out of step with representations of masculine comportment in other national literary traditions: the masculinist hubris he demonstrates may be of an extreme type, but there are many more extreme examples of misogyny in British fiction published simultaneously with *Things Fall Apart*. The sexually ruthless Joe Lampton in John Braine's *Room at the Top* (1957) or Alan Sillitoe's Arthur Seaton in *Saturday Night and Sunday Morning* (1958), for example. In fact, more than once in *A Man of the People*, Odili's blatant philandering is conveyed with the same wry debased humour as that which characterizes Jim Dixon in Kingsley Amis's *Lucky Jim* (1954). After cogitating on 'the trouble with our new nation', Odili swiftly adds, 'Needless to say I did not spend the entire night on these elevated thoughts. Most of the time my mind was on Elsie, so much so in fact that I had to wake up in the middle of the night and change my pyjama trousers' (*MP* 37). In 'Girls at War', Reginald Nwankwo from the Ministry of Justice is stopped at the Awka checkpoint in Biafra by a girl to whom he once gave career advice. He has been insistent that girls are not required in the militia, scoffing at their revolutionary zeal (the prime joke among his friends at the beginning of the war is a contingent of girls from a local secondary school marching behind a banner: 'WE ARE IMPREGNABLE!'). At first he fails to realize that women are capable of making any contribution to the war effort at all. Achebe makes him representative of a misogynist tendency for which the war is only a pretext: Gladys finds herself oscillating from soldier to civilian, the kept woman of some privileged officer or of a black-market trader made powerful by the war ('That is what you men want us to do'). Despite beginning his own affair with Gladys, Nwankwo holds himself above her; he is repulsed by the common parlance whereby sex is 'shelling' and contraception prevents the 'pouring in' of the 'troops', even as he uses the young woman. Significantly, in 1972 Achebe attempted to tackle the precarious gender politics of war. Gladys is the pivot of his argument here: as Nwankwo comes to acknowledge, she is positioned as 'a mirror reflecting a society that had gone completely rotten and maggoty at the centre', only to end in 'tears and blood' (*GW* 110).

As early as 1952, while a student at Ibadan, Achebe published, in the *University Herald*, a story which some twenty years later he retitled and included in the collection *Girls at War*. In this story, Achebe explores the ways in which fundamentalist Christian belief is confining to women. Nnaemeke (like Obi in *No Longer at Ease*) returns from Lagos

101

to his father's home to tell him of his engagement to be married. When he explains his fiancée is a teacher, his father is quick to scoff: 'Teacher did you say? If you consider that a qualification for a good wife I should like to point out to you, that no Christian woman should teach. St Paul in his letter to the Corinthians says that women should keep silence' (GW 23). The father's prejudices extend beyond gender since the wife his son has chosen is 'no Christian' either and he debars himself from seeing his son's family for many, many years. It is a letter from his daughter-in-law that finally breaks through the stalemate between father and son. Writing with a feminist consciousness can be more clearly attributed to Sembene Ousmane who, as early as 1960, in *God's Bits of Wood*, represents politically active women striking alongside male railway workers and, in *Xala* (1974), studies the effects of polygamy on women's civil rights; yet Achebe did not lack concern in his early work.

It has clearly been left to African women writers (Ama Ata Aidoo in *Our Sister Killjoy*, 1977, and Mariama Bâ in *So Long A Letter*, 1981, for example), to excavate neocolonial and patriarchal societies following Independence.[17] The history of postcolonial policies which disadvantage women, while deeply implicated in colonialism is not reducible to it, as Mariama Bâ carefully demonstrates in her fiction. But in 1962 Achebe turned his attention to the gender biases of traditional Igbo mores in the short story 'Akueke'. The young Igbo girl of the title is alienated by her brothers who are irritated that she has the gall to dismiss marriage suitors. They begin to believe she is suffering from a dangerous illness that portends she should die, and she is abandoned in the Evil Forest. She survives and seeks refuge with her maternal grandfather who in his wisdom castigates his grandsons, removing their sister, changing her name and taking her into his home where, it is implied, she shall be granted more control over her life. C. L. Innes, one of the few scholars to consider Achebe's short stories in real depth, wonders whether Akueke suffers 'a psychosomatic illness, like the illnesses suffered by so many European women in the nineteenth century, as a means of resisting the intolerable demands of a patriarchal society'.[18] Certainly, she is correct in her judgement elsewhere that, in the stories, Achebe

102

deliberately concentrates on those who have become marginalized or outcasts in Nigerian society and who fail to secure chief roles in his novels: 'the women, the children, the clerks, the poor traders and craftsmen – and [Achebe] also focuses a much harsher light on those who exploit or ignore them, the complacent middle-class professionals'.[19] This is exactly what underlies Achebe's representations of women in *Anthills of the Savannah* and there is some evidence of a movement in this direction in earlier fiction. Florence Stratton takes up Achebe's representations of women and locates him centrally within her disquisition on gender and African writing. She begins by rereading *Things Fall Apart* alongside Ifi Amadiume's *Male Daughters, Female Husbands* (1987), a revisionist history of Igbo gender relations, in order to uncover the occlusions in the text with regard to women. Later, in a chapter entitled 'Gender on the Agenda', she acknowledges the ways in which Achebe revises his representations in *Anthills of the Savannah*, but provides a thorough critique of the functions to which Beatrice and Elewa are put – especially the latter, 'Ikem's girl', whose primary function is to bear the child who will follow 'The Shining Path of Ikem'.[20]

During an interview conducted in 1994, the year that Stratton published her study, Achebe stated that the book he intended to write next would concentrate on women characters: 'From time to time in his culture, when things have gone wrong, he says, women have risen up to take action'. Achebe cited one such time in the 1950s that might prove a dramatic source (earlier in 1990 he also expressed his interest in writing about the Aba Women's Uprising of 1929).[21] What he omitted to discuss was the attention women characters had already received in *Anthills of the Savannah* where he privileges gender over other forms of oppression that receive attention in his literary model for social change. Beatrice Okoh is patently Achebe's most memorable woman character and, as Innes was first to point out, he leads us to read Beatrice as his mouthpiece. Articulate and iconic, she is also damaged by the experience and Achebe does not leave her to carry the burden of experience alone. As Stratton asserts, he moves other female figures into the narrative formerly occupied by the failed male trinity of Ikem, Chris and Sam: Elewa and Elewa's baby

Amaechina, a girl with a boy's name. They are the cornerstones on which an alternative politics must be built. The end of the novel leaves women at the forefront of social and national struggle if not yet in the political powerhouse.

Soyinka's *A Dance of the Forests*, a play commissioned to celebrate Nigeria's Independence in 1960, has at its centre an *abiku*, a half-formed child, symbolic of the, then, half-formed nation. It is an image to which Ben Okri returns in 1991 in *The Famished Road* and which Achebe notes when he points out that Christopher Okigbo has been compared to an *ogbanje*, the reincarnated child of Igbo tradition. More than any other writer, Chinua Achebe has conveyed the changing fortunes of the half-formed nation to readers around the world. It is clear to Achebe and, borrowing his clarity, it becomes clear to the reader that the Nigerian national situation must acquire sharper contours. *Anthills of the Savannah* does not provide sharp contours but conforms to Fredric Jameson's well-known formulation of a socially symbolic text. Achebe might argue, like Ikem, that 'Writers don't give prescriptions ... They give headaches' (*AS* 161). Ikem tells Beatrice that women themselves must claim and then define their role in the nation: '*You have to tell us. We never asked you before*' (*AS* 92). Achebe sets the mood but not the agenda.[22]

Since 1987 Achebe has not published another novel. He is a public intellectual who continues to lecture, to teach and to write essays. When asked whether he will compose a novel, this time set in the United States where he has lived most recently, he typically responds by dismissing an idea that does not centre his creative talent on Nigeria. Achebe maintains that America has sufficient novelists to write about the nation while Nigeria still has too few. The etymological evolution from 'tribe' to 'nation' is also a political construction in which Achebe has been very heavily involved: 'Nothing in Nigeria's political history captures her problem of national integration more graphically than the chequered fortune of the word tribe' (*TN* 5).

Writing is for Achebe an ideological act, as he has explained time and again over his long career. In 'Africa and her Writers' (1972), he states that art serves the needs of the times and of society ('Art for art's sake is just another kind of deodorised dog-shit', *MYCD* 19). The invective is wry, thrown out for effect but the sentiment remains unchanged over some fifty years. Achebe is a writer raised in an *mbari* culture for whom Africa is a metaphysical literary landscape as well as 'home', and in *Anthills of the Savannah* his imaginative powers are given full rein. A felt irony in this novel is that the leadership is made sufficiently intelligent to have analysed the national situation and to have circumvented many of their failures, like their failure to encompass women in their ideas of new nation. The ruling elite has made the fatal assumption that the public remains largely unconscious of 'the trouble with Nigeria'.

6

Conclusion: 'A Book Bound in Flesh and Blood'

I am the sole witness to my homecoming.

(Christopher Okigbo, 'Distances', 1964)

In concluding this assessment of Achebe's work, it is apposite to return to the idea of 'story', that which animates Nigeria's grand old man of letters. Achebe always tells stories of 'home', even when his distance from Nigeria is great; Nigeria is, he says, the 'ambience' in which his 'awakening story' came into being. He remains vigilantly Nigerian and, I argue in this final chapter, as his stories trace Nigeria's ideological shift from tribe to nation, Achebe has become a far more political writer than is often recognized. Here I draw on examples of Achebe's writerly responsibility to Nigeria and explore the idea that, just as he returns 'home' in his writing, writers and critics from around the world continually return to his novels and essays in theirs.

Achebe has described man as 'a story-making animal': 'He rarely passes up an opportunity to accompany his works and his experiences with matching stories' and he argues that the historical fact of repossession needs 'enabling stories' (*HE* 59). In *Anthills of the Savannah*, a character declares that the story 'saves our progeny from blundering like blind beggars into the spikes of the cactus fence. The story is our escort; without it we are blind ... it is the story that owns us and directs us' (*AS* 200). Achebe's critical position on the salience of storytelling as a cultural tool pre-empts similar more theorized discussions of the role and function of literature. In 'The Novelist as Teacher', an essay he wrote in 1965, Achebe asserted that fiction could provide a handle on reality and he has reiterated this position ever since, maintaining that literature enables readers to 'encounter in the safe, manageable dimensions of make-believe the very same threats to integrity that may assail the psyche in real life' (*HI* 96). Fredric Jameson is perhaps best known for his extrapolation on narrative as a socially symbolic act in which 'real social contradictions, insurmountable in their own terms' are allowed 'a purely formal resolution' in the text.[1] Although the emphasis on the political and social function of stories and storytelling may appear utopian, in a 1991 interview Achebe has continued to assert 'the story is like the genes that are transferred to create the new being. It is far more important than anything else'.[2]

Achebe has lived away from his home in Ogidi, Anambra State, for many years. He has told stories of armed soldiers coming to seek him out at Nigeria's Broadcasting House in order to discover whether their guns were indeed mightier than the pen of the writer of *A Man of the People*. Achebe's satire of 1966 is a classic example of life imitating art because the military coup he imagined and the coup that actually took place are uncannily similar. The novel was published the very same week of the coup. Achebe was forced to follow the rest of his family in returning to his home village as the massacres of Igbos signalled the beginning of civil war. He says:

> I found it difficult to forgive Nigeria and my countrymen and women for the political nonchalance and cruelty that unleashed upon us these terrible events which set us back a whole generation and robbed us of the chance to become a medium rank developed nation in the 20th century.[3]

It is clearly very important to Achebe that any exile be honourable. He did not flee Nigeria but remained long enough after the coup, 'to receive whatever retribution might be due to me for renouncing Nigeria' for the thirty-month period of civil war. When a general amnesty ensued, he set out for America where he has spent many years on and off. Returning home, he has said 'I don't consider that I have any right to seek out a more comfortable corner of the world' (*TN* 10), but circumstances have not always favoured living at home. He left

Nigeria again when in 1990 a road accident in Lagos left him paralysed from the waist down. He left in order to ensure that the needs of his medical condition could be met, first in England and later in the United States, something that the Nigerian hospital system could not guarantee.

In examining issues of home and exile, it is important to differentiate between nomad and indigene, between the global cosmopolitan (the 'restless artist-in-exile' epitomized by Salman Rushdie and defined in Edward Said's discussion of the migratory writer) and the fearful and embattled refugee, often from the world's poorest and wartorn places, who is coerced into exile. While for Rushdie roots are 'a conservative myth, designed to keep us in our places', Achebe's roots in Nigeria prefigure each and every word he continues to write.[4] He fits neither the paradigmatic formulas of the artistically free exile nor the persecuted political writer. Rather, his position is bound up in the idea of home: the desire to leave and the longing to return. African American poet Countee Cullen asked the deceptively complex question, 'What is Africa to me?' and Achebe has never stopped turning over that same vexed question: what is Nigeria to a man and a writer who, even when he lives at a distance looking back from a more comfortable corner, is ever vigilant about his country. In 1989 in an interview for the *Nigerian Statesman* he described himself as 'a missionary in reverse' (perhaps echoing Caribbean writer Louise Bennett's mischievously ironic poem 'Colonization in Reverse'). He has offered a wry explanation:

> The whole purpose of African literature in my view is to change the perception of the world as far as Africans are concerned, and for me that's being a missionary. So I have been very busy spreading the good news that Africans are people, that we are not savages and cannibals.[5]

In his early writing Achebe seems embattled rather than reconciliatory. It is a long road from *Things Fall Apart* to *Anthills of the Savannah*. The journey involves the etymological evolution from 'tribe' to 'nation', a construction in which Achebe has been heavily involved. Tribe is an item in the lexicon of colonial discourse bequeathed to the colonized and Achebe relinquishes the word, espousing 'nation' instead (*HE*

5). Like the eminent historian of Africa Basil Davidson, he deplores those who 'retreat into tribe' (*TN* 5) or take 'the advantage which tribalism may confer on mediocrity' (*TN* 19). In his literary work, 'nation' too remains a slippery term, largely because of what Anthony Smith describes as the 'two poles of *ethnie* and state which it seeks to subsume and transcend'.[6] Nigeria's failure to negotiate between the two taxes Achebe more as the years pass and translates into his fiction as the balancing of stories about the past with those about the unsettled present.

Achebe is a writer who has travelled the world speaking his mind. He admired James Baldwin precisely for his ability to say 'the emperor has no clothes' despite becoming unpopular with the emperor.[7] He has lived for long periods in America and given numerous talks designed to promote cultural exchange, challenging the West, and the United States in particular, to be more open to different cultural ideas and traditions: 'It's not as if the world were closed. You are self-contained. It's dangerous if in addition to being the policeman of the world you're trying to control, you make the wrong decisions based on insufficient knowledge'.[8] Time and again Achebe has charged Nigeria with the same mistaken tendency to be inward-looking. As a social critic Achebe has been most vociferous in his defence of open dialogue between nations and continents. Achebe is a far more political writer than critics who compare him with Wole Soyinka or Ngugi Wa Thiong'o tend to allow. Comments on the Nigerian government's hypocrisy resulted in the banning of his books from schools and colleges in 1987 and Lagos State University's rescinding of their decision to award him an honorary doctorate only twenty-four hours prior to the convocation. Such slights may be of little import for a writer as internationally acclaimed as Achebe, but they serve to reinforce his role as eloquent conscience for a society. Achebe continues to annotate each development in Nigeria's national story: 'The day I lose hope in Nigeria, I will stop talking about it'.[9]

By the end of the twentieth century, as one critic pointed out, 'you can say "Okonkwo" from Liberia to Kenya and down to Swaziland, and people with a high school education or more will recognize the proud, fierce, tragic hero of *Things Fall*

Apart'.[10] What James North omits to consider is how many more readers will also acknowledge his impact on their personal reading as well as his (re)shaping of African literature. Achebe is a rare writer whose very first foray into fiction became an instant classic. It is also rare for a writer to catch the imaginations of so many readers in completely different, and sometimes contradictory, national and geographical contexts, and to maintain his hold over them. Nelson Mandela famously read Achebe's novels while in prison. He has described Achebe as a freedom fighter, the one writer who 'made the prison walls come tumbling down'. David. N. Dinkins, the first African American mayor of New York City proclaimed 25 May 1989 Chinua Achebe Day in honour of the writer's 'expression and transmission of knowledge and truth' while lecturing at City University.[11]

Maya Jaggi reporting on Achebe's 70th birthday celebrations in 2000 reels off an impressive list of those who sent tributes. Many of these accolades came from fellow writers who have been consistent in their praise of Achebe for many years: Africans – Wole Soyinka and Nadine Gordimer – and African Americans – Toni Morrison and John Edgar Wideman. Mandela, Kofi Annan, Secretary-General of United Nations, and Olusegun Obasanjo, the current Nigerian leader and the first civilian president for almost twenty years also celebrated his birthday.[12] Achebe's literary influence bridges different cultures and political contexts, witness P. Nadakumar's essay on Achebe in the New Delhi publication *The Glory and the Good: Essays in Literature* (1965) and Edna Aizenberg's comparison of Achebe and Latin American Julio Cortazar, through to collections like *South Asian Responses to Chinua Achebe* (1993). Achebe's biographer, Ezenwa-Ohaeto, tells a story of a class at a university in South Korea who wrote to Achebe to tell him his depiction of the British colonization of Nigeria had enhanced their understanding of the Japanese colonization of Korea.[13]

More than forty years after the publication of *Things Fall Apart*, Achebe remains a key focus of African literary criticism; it is indeed still 'morning yet on creation day' as far as responses to his work are concerned. Achebe remains focused, too, on the idea of postcolonial writing as a rebuttal, as this study has shown. He is continually engaged in dialogue with egregious colonial stories that, in his view, will persist into the new millennium. This is not to suggest that Achebe is stymied by a dogged insistence on single-issue political writing but to detect in even the most recent essays, like the lectures collected as *Home and Exile*, that he maintains the sharp moral edge for which he first became known, and to recognize that this often makes him an uncompromisingly clear-sighted writer. In *Home and Exile*, Achebe berates Joyce Cary for the 'undertow of uncharitableness' and the 'distaste, hatred and mockery' that 'poison' his tales of Africa (*HE* 24) and continues to draw his readers' attention to the circumlocutory unintelligibility of the classic *Heart of Darkness*.

Identifying what he sees as Conrad's betrayal of anti-imperialist principles in the novel and the blindspots of Conrad's critics, Achebe succeeded in opening up discussions of colonial ideology as it affects the writing and reading of literature as long ago as 1975. Writers and critics, James North and poet Craig Raine, for example, regularly revisit Achebe's argument[14] and he has continued to pursue ideas of writerly responsibility even in a poststructuralist literary climate in which such ideas are often dismissed. He refutes the vagaries of literary-critical fashion for old-fashioned ethics. For example, in *Home and Exile*, he turns to V. S. Naipaul. Recipient of the Nobel Prize in 2001, Naipaul has long been a controversial figure for those who resent his negative portrayals of India in *An Area of Darkness* (1964), and of disillusioned migrants in *The Mimic Men* (1987). Often considered Conrad's literary heir, Naipaul revisits Conrad's Congo in his bleak 'African novel', *A Bend in the River* (1979). His literary exploration of emergent postcolonial Africa according to many postcolonial critics sinks into an anthropological trivialization of African cultures and civilizations. The extent to which a novel like *A Bend in the River* engages as it outrages keeps returning critics to Achebe's original discussion of *Heart of Darkness* and to Achebe's facility for providing what Edward Said values in *Culture and Imperialism* (1993): contrapuntal readings of texts that acknowledge their permeability and the intertwining histories of the former colonizers with those formerly colonized. A further example is Joan Didion's *Salvador* (1983), a politically self-conscious text in which Conrad's novella also serves as the interpretative grid.

111

Allusions abound in Didion's work, usually extrapolating on Central America's inexpressibility and untranslatability. Salvador (with a 'frontier proximity to the cultural zero') is made the more ambivalent by Didion's recourse to the ur-text that is the embedded centre of Achebe's literary critical output. It is difficult to read *A Bend in the River* or *Salvador* without recourse to the dynamic critical model that Achebe has put in place. Indeed, in *Palace of the Peacock* (1960), Guyanese writer Wilson Harris extends *Heart of Darkness* to unlock an 'incomplete' text whose parodic possibilities remain trapped in a moribund imperialism. Harris's creative resistance and intervention into *Heart of Darkness* underlines the fact that Achebe's literary criticism has been a significant point of departure for a series of novelists and critics.

Achebe's immersion in what he sees as an inevitable link between writing and politics has ensured his place as a primary spokesman for Africa's autochthonous population. In *Anthills of the Savannah*, Beatrice asks a question that Achebe wrestles with time and again, especially in his fiction: 'What must a people do to appease an embittered history?' (*AS* 220). Nigeria has embraced its own bitter colonial legacy and Achebe's fiction grapples with the problems contingent upon its failures in twentieth-century world politics. Nevertheless, what Achebe repeatedly refers to in his most recent collection, *Home and Exile*, is 'an African homecoming celebration'. Although there seems little cause to be sanguine about Nigeria, Achebe's definition of home is elucidating:

> my home was under attack and ... my home was not merely a house or a town but, more importantly, an awakening story in whose ambience my own existence had first begun to assemble its fragments into a coherence and meaning ... over which, even today ... I still do not have sufficient mastery, but about which I can say one thing: that it is not the same story Joyce Cary intended me to have (*HE* 38).

Exile implies the absence of home, but Achebe has cumulatively constructed a shifting national allegory in which pre- and post-colonial Nigeria has interiority: Achebe is composing and re-composing Nigeria wherever he is, Africa, Europe or America, in lectures or in fiction. Toni Morrison has explored

112

the idea of home as 'psychically and physically safe'.[15] Nigeria may have been neither of these things for Achebe but, following the road accident that left him paralysed, Achebe was astonished by the waves of sympathy that enveloped him from Nigerians of all political and religious persuasions, 'The hard words that Nigeria and I have said to each other begin to look like anxious words of love, not hate'.[16] Though Achebe may express surprise, in 1987 he had also been awarded Nigeria's prestigious National Merit Award, designed to honour the intellectual achievements of a respected citizen. Such accolades – and this one was awarded despite Achebe's residence away from Nigeria for much of the preceding decade – are testament to his facility for telling Nigerian stories that are also 'home truths'. The surprise Achebe has expressed at his continued cultural pre-eminence in his homeland may result from his tendency to season his Nigerian stories with salt. The Igbo narrative tradition places value on the narrator 'putting salt here and there in his story' and R. N. Egudu has explained that salt represents 'verisimilitude or fabulous or folkloric anecdotes'.[17] Achebe's stories sometimes also reverberate with the kind of sharpness that some might see as pouring salt into the nation's many wounds: Achebe never lets up in his call for a fairer, collective social order.

After his car crash in March of 1990, Nigerian newspapers published pages and pages of messages from readers wishing Achebe a speedy recovery. One such message read, 'We nearly lost a book bound in flesh and blood'.[18] These simple words offered by one of Achebe's readers are a fitting description of a writer whose career began by writing back to those who forged 'fake title deeds' (HE 68) for African literature and who wrested back empire stories, spinning new ones to tell a century's worth of tales about his home.

Notes

CHAPTER 1. INTRODUCTION: WRITING FOR RECOVERY

1. Igbo is sometimes spelled Ibo. It is the name of the people and of their language.
2. See, for example, Frantz Fanon, *The Wretched of the Earth* (London: Penguin, 1990).
3. Simon Gikandi discussing Eustace Palmer, in *Reading Chinua Achebe: Language and Ideology in Fiction* (Portsmouth, NH: Heinemann, 1991), 105.
4. Kwame Nkrumah, *Neo-Colonialism: The Last Stage of Imperialism* (London: Nelson, 1965).
5. Stuart Hall, 'Cultural Identity and Diaspora', in Jonathan Rutherford (ed.), *Identity: Community, Culture, Difference* (London: Lawrence and Wishart, 1990), 225.
6. Franco Moretti, 'The Spell of Indecision', in Cary Nelson and Larry Grossberg (eds.), *Marxism and the Interpretation of Culture* (Urbana: University of Illinois, 1988), 344.
7. Wole Soyinka, 'From a Common Backcloth: A Reassessment of the African Literary Image' (1963), in *Art, Dialogue and Outrage: Essays on Literature and Culture* (London: Methuen, 1993), 11; Soyinka in 'The Patriot as Artist': 'When the writer in his own society can no longer function as a conscience, he must recognise that his choice lies between denying himself totally or *withdrawing to the position of chronicler* and post-mortem surgeon' (my emphasis), in G. D. Killam (ed.), *African Writers on African Writing* (London: Heinemann, 1973), 89.
8. See Kole Omotoso, *Achebe or Soyinka? A Study in Contrasts* (London: Hans Zell, 1996).
9. See Walter J. Ong, *Orality and Literacy: The Technologizing of the Word* (London: Routledge, 1989).

10. For example, Abiole Irele, *The African Experience in Language and Ideology* (Bloomington: Indiana University Press, 1990); Georg M. Gugelberger, *Marxism and African Literature* (Trenton, NJ: Africa World Press, 1985).

11. For further exploration of this idea, see, for example, Graham Holderness, Bryan Loughrey and Nahem Yousaf, *George Orwell* (London: Macmillan, 1998).

12. Stanley Macebah, interviewed on the *South Bank Show*, London Weekend Television, January 1990.

13. Achebe, in a letter in the *Nigeria English Studies Association Bulletin*, 1 (1966), 9 as quoted by Felicity Riddy, 'Language as a Theme in *No Longer at Ease*', in C. L. Innes and Bernth Lindfors (eds.), *Critical Perspectives on Chinua Achebe* (London: Heinemann, 1978), 150; Chinua Achebe, 'The Role of the Writer in the New Nation', *Nigeria Magazine*, 81 (1964), 160.

14. Achebe, quoted in Ezenwa-Ohaeto, *Chinua Achebe* (Oxford: James Currey, 1997), 87.

15. Chinweizu, 'Introduction: Redrawing the Map of African Literature', in *Voices in Twentieth-Century Africa: Griots and Towncriers* (London: Faber, 1988), xvii–xl.

16. C. L. Innes, Introduction in Innes and Lindfors, *Critical Perspectives*, 6; Kofi Awonoor, *The Breast of the Earth* (New York: Doubleday, 1975), 280.

17. Cosmo Pieterse and Donald Munro, *Protest and Conflict in African Literature* (London: Heinemann, 1969), ix.

18. Alhaji Sir Abubakar Tafawa Balewa, *Shaihu Umar*, trans. Mervin Hiskett (New York: Markus Wiener Publishing Inc., 1989). The first American edition uses Hiskett's 1967 translation as published by Longman, Green and Co.

19. Some of the Onitsha stories are anthologized in Emmanuel Obiechina's introduction, *Onitsha Market Literature* (London: Heinemann, 1972), and others form the Appendix to Obiechina's *An African Popular Literature: A Study of Onitsha Market Pamphlets* (Cambridge: Cambridge University Press, 1973). Achebe's Foreword to the latter is also reprinted in *Morning Yet on Creation Day*, 90–2.

20. Jonathan A. Peters, 'English-Language Fiction from West Africa', in Oyekan Owomoyela (ed.), *A History of Twentieth-Century African Literatures* (Lincoln: University of Nebraska Press, 1993), 9–48.

21. Chinua Achebe, 'The Role of the Writer', 157.

22. Mariama Bâ, *So Long a Letter* (London: Virago, 1987), 42.

23. Gikandi, *Reading Chinua Achebe*, 110.

115

24. See Mikhail Bakhtin, 'Epic and Novel', in M. M. Bakhtin, *The Dialogic Imagination*, ed. M. Holquist, trans. C. Emerson and M. Holquist (Austin, TX: University of Texas Press), 1–40.
25. Gareth Griffiths, 'Chinua Achebe: When Did You Last See Your Father?' *World Literature Written in English*, 27:1 (1987), 18–27.

CHAPTER 2. THE TROUBLE WITH EUROPE: WRITING BACK

1. Wole Soyinka, *South Bank Show*, London Weekend Television, January 1990.
2. See Elaine Showalter's exploration of this idea in 'King Romance', in *Sexual Anarchy: Gender and Culture at the Fin de Siècle* (London: Virago, 1992), 76–104.
3. H. Rider Haggard, *She* (Oxford: World's Classics, 1992), 273.
4. See Joseph Bristow, *Empire Boys: Adventures in a Man's World* (London: HarperCollins, 1991) for a discussion of boys' papers and the unifying ideology of imperialism they promulgated for their readers.
5. Abdul JanMohamed, 'The Economy of Manichean Allegory: The Function of Racial Difference in Colonialist Literature', *Critical Inquiry*, 12 (Autumn 1985), 64.
6. Joseph Conrad, *Heart of Darkness* (London: Penguin, 1981).
7. Conrad, *Heart of Darkness*, 10.
8. Cedric Watts, ' "A Bloody Racist": About Achebe's Views on Conrad', *Yearbook of English Studies*, 1983, 196–209.
9. Ngugi quoted in C. P. Sarvan, 'Racism and the *Heart of Darkness*', in Robert Kimbrough (ed.), *Heart of Darkness* (New York: Norton, 1988), 262–8 and 280–85; D. C. R. A. Goonetilleke, 'Ironies of Progress: Joseph Conrad and Imperialism in Africa', in Robert Giddings (ed.), *Literature and Imperialism* (Macmillan: London, 1991), 86; Felix Mnthali, 'Continuity and Change in Conrad and Ngugi', *Kunapipi*, 3:1 (1981), 83.
10. Anthony Fothergill, 'Of Conrad, Cannibals and Kin', in Mick Gidley (ed.), *Representing Others: White Views of Indigenous Peoples* (Exeter: University of Exeter Press, 1992), 49. Benita Parry, in *Conrad and Imperialism: Ideological Boundaries and Visionary Frontiers* (London: Macmillan, 1983), notes that Conrad disliked Haggard's and Buchan's work but 'his own fictions with their racial stereotypes, ingratiating generalities on alien customs and the native mind, and their tendency to attach moral valuations to cultural particularities, do have affinities with writings he despised' (p. 2).

11. Conrad, *Heart of Darkness*, 7.
12. If a variation on the scholarly Holly exists in *Heart of Darkness*, it is in the person of the 'artist' Kurtz: ' "He is a prodigy" he said at last. "He is an emissary of pity, and science and progress, and devil knows what else" ' (p. 36). This assessment by the brick-maker casts Kurtz in the light of a cosmopolitan intellectual (his name is German, he serves the Belgian empire, he speaks English to Marlow); he is a 'universal genius', if we, like Marlow, accept Kurtz's cousin's assertion (p. 103). But Conrad, deconstructing the potential hero at the centre of the text, makes him a demonic figure in whom the best and the worst of his epoch and continent are brought face to face with their own parodic reflection.
13. I see *Heart of Darkness* as belonging to the early phase of modernism, but the novella's form can still be seen to retain elements of a realist framework in documenting the river journey, and of the romance in its negotiated connection with the genre of the 'imperial romance'. Conrad comments wryly on the critics' quandary in defining literary form: 'I have been called a romantic. Well it can't be helped. But stay. I seem to remember that I have been called a realist also' (Joseph Conrad, *A Personal Record* (London: J. M. Dent & Sons, 1975, 111). See also Michael Bell (ed.), *The Context of English Literature 1900–1930* (London: Methuen, 1980), where Bell reads Conrad as one 'who partake(s) of the broader tendencies of modernist literature yet respond(s) to the world in a manner consonant with the techniques and assumptions of realist fiction' (p. 67).
14. Conrad, *Heart of Darkness*, 30.
15. F. R. Leavis, *The Great Tradition* (London: Penguin, 1986), 204; Conrad, *Heart of Darkness*, 23.
16. Patrick Brantlinger, '*Heart of Darkness*: Anti-Imperialism, Racism, or Impressionism?', *Criticism*, 27:4 (Fall 1985), 363–85; Fredric Jameson, *The Political Unconscious* (London: Methuen, 1985).
17. Frantz Fanon, *Black Skin, White Masks* (London: Pluto, 1986).
18. Parry, *Conrad and Imperialism*, 22–3.
19. Achebe, quoted in Enzenma-Olaeto, 259.
20. Ironically, Bruce Beresford's film *Mister Johnson* (1990), adapted from Cary's novel by novelist William Boyd, was the first international feature film shot in Nigeria. Maynard Eziashi who played Mister Johnson became the first black British actor to win an international award (the Best Actor Bear at the Berlin Film Festival).
21. Joyce Cary, *Mister Johnson* (London: Penguin, 1980), 23–4.
22. Conrad, *Heart of Darkness*, 52.

23. C. L. Innes, *Chinua Achebe* (Cambridge: Cambridge University Press, 1990), 22.

24. Abdul JanMohamed, 'The Generation of the Racial Romance', in *Manichean Aesthetics: The Politics of Literature in Colonial Africa* (Amherst: University of Massachusetts Press, 1983), 40.

25. James Currey, Alan Hill and Keith Sambrook in conversation with Kirsten Holst Petersen, 'Working with Chinua Achebe: The African Writers Series', in Kirsten Holst Petersen and Anna Rutherford, *Chinua Achebe: A Celebration* (Porstmouth, NH: Heinemann, 1991), 149–59. Much of the information in this section derives from this fascinating interview.

26. Alan Hill, in 'Working with Chinua Achebe', 152.

27. Bill Moyers, 'Interview with Chinua Achebe', in *A World of Ideas*, ed. Betty Sue Flowers (New York: Doubleday, 1985), 343.

28. Somini Sengupta, 'Chinua Achebe: A Literary Diaspora Toasts One of its Own'. Sengupta is a journalist for the *New York Times* and the 2000 article can be accessed at <http://www.usaafricaonline.com/achebe70.html>.

CHAPTER 3. THE PAST IS ANOTHER COUNTRY: *THINGS FALL APART* AND *ARROW OF GOD*

1. Chinua Achebe, 'The Role of the New Writer in a New Nation', *Nigeria Magazine*, 81 (1964), 157.

2. Wole Soyinka, *Myth, Literature and the African World* (Cambridge: Cambridge University Press, 1978), 92.

3. See Chidi Amuta, *The Theory of African Literature: Implications for Practical Criticism* (London: Zed, 1989).

4. Mineke Schipper, *Beyond the Boundaries: African Literature and Literary Theory* (London: Allison and Busby, 1989), 162.

5. Abdul JanMohamed, 'The Economy of Manichean Allegory: The Function of Racial Difference in Colonialist Literature', *Critical Inquiry*, 12:1 (1985), 62.

6. Edward Said uncovers the discourse of empire inscribed not only in overtly empire writing but outside of it in canonical texts. In *Culture and Imperialism* (London: Chatto and Windus, 1993) he provides close readings of *Mansfield Park* and *Jane Eyre* as imperial texts where imperialism is 'the practice, the theory and the attitude of a dominating metropolitan centre ruling a distant territory'. See also Gayatri Spivak, 'Three Women's Texts and a Critique of Imperialism', *Critical Inquiry*, 12 (Autumn 1985),

241–61; Moira Ferguson, '*Mansfield Park*: Slavery, Colonialism and Gender', *Oxford Literary Review*, 13 (1991), 118–39.

7. Achebe defines *mbari* in 'Africa and Her Writers', in *Morning Yet on Creation Day*, and in his South Bank lecture of 1990 published as 'African Literature as Restoration of Celebration' in Kirsten Holst Petersen and Anna Rutherford, *Chinua Achebe: A Celebration* (Portsmouth, NH: Heinemann, 1991), 1–10.

8. Simon Gikandi points out that a similar duality is also embodied in the concept of the *chi*, the Igbo marketplace and various other metaphors. See *Reading Chinua Achebe: Language and Ideology in Fiction* (Portsmouth, NH: Heinemann, 1991), 20.

9. Simon Gikandi reads the novel as a sustained struggle for power which is characterized by significant moments in which Achebe deploys the figure of the dancing mask. See *Reading Chinua Achebe*, 51–77.

10. Mikhail Bakhtin, 'Discourse in the Novel', in *The Dialogic Imagination*, ed. Michael Holquist, trans. Michael Holquist and Caryl Emerson (Austin: University of Texas Press, 1981), 293.

11. Gerald Moore, *Seven African Writers* (London: Oxford University Press, 1972), 58–9; Robert Serumaga, 'A Mirror of Integration: Chinua Achebe and James Ngugi', in Cosmo Pieterse and Donald Munro, *Protest and Conflict in African Literature* (London: Heinemann, 1969), 76.

12. See, for example, Josef Schmied, 'The English Language and African Identities', *The Cambridge Review*, June 1990, 57–60.

13. Leon Botstein, 'Things Fall Together: A Conversation with Chinua Achebe and Toni Morrison', *Transition: An International Review*, 11:1 (2001), 157.

14. Chris Dutton, 'Review of *Hopes and Impediments, Selected Essays 1964–1987*', in *West Africa*, 12–18 (September 1998), 1675.

15. Botstein, 'A Conversation with Chinua Achebe', 150–65.

16. See Charles Nnolim, 'A Source for *Arrow of God*' and C. L. Innes's 'Response' in C. L. Innes and Bernth Lindfors (eds.), *Critical Perspectives on Chinua Achebe* (London: Heinemann, 1978), 219–45.

17. Chinua Achebe, *South Bank Show*, London Weekend Television, January 1990.

18. Benedict Anderson, *Imagined Communities: Reflections on the Origin and Spread of Nationalism* (1983; rev. edn. London: Verso, 1990), 110. Anderson is discussing the role of colonial school systems in promoting nationalisms.

CHAPTER 4. POLITICIANS, PIONEERS, PRODIGAL SONS: *NO LONGER AT EASE* AND *A MAN OF THE PEOPLE*

1. For Saro-Wiwa' s story, see *A Month and a Day: A Detention Diary* by *Ken Saro-Wiwa* (London: Penguin, 1995). Wole Soyinka, quoted in John Vidal, 'Writing Wrongs', *Guardian*, 2 November 1995.
2. See Homi Bhabha, *The Location of Culture* (London: Routledge, 1993).
3. Frantz Fanon, *The Wretched of the Earth* (London, Penguin, 1990), 200.
4. Wole Soyinka, 'From a Common Backcloth: A Reassessment of the African Literary Image' (1966), in *Art, Dialogue and Outrage: Essays on Literature and Culture* (London: Methuen, 1993), 11.
5. Here I am borrowing Michel Pecheux's notion of counteridentification (turning derogatory images back on those who promulgate them) and disidentification (transforming those images). For an explanation in relation to postcolonial fictions, see Bill Ashcroft, Gareth Griffiths and Helen Tiffin, *The Empire Writes Back: Theory and Practice in Post-Colonial Literatures* (London: Routledge, 1989), 170–73.
6. Simon Gikandi, *Reading Chinua Achebe: Language and Ideology in Fiction* (Portsmouth, NH: Heinemann, 1991), 79.
7. Eustace Palmer, *An Introduction to the African Novel* (London: Heinemann, 1971), 63. G. D. Killam thinks similarly in this case and is representative of the Achebe scholars who believe that he is more successful writing epic struggles than contemporary critiques; see *The Novels of Chinua Achebe* (London: Heinemann, 1969).
8. For Abdul JanMohamed, the phase that follows the 'dominant' phase of colonization is the 'hegemonic' phase by which time the colonized have internalized the colonial system; see 'The Economy of Manichean Allegory: the Function of Racial Difference in Colonialist literature', *Critical Inquiry*, 12:1 (Autumn 1985), 59–87.
9. Chinua Achebe, 'The Role of the Writer in a New Nation', in *Nigeria Magazine*, 81 (1964), 157.
10. In his classic *The Country and the City* (1973), Raymond Williams praises *Things Fall Apart* for its portrayal of a rural community in the process of change, but he does not move beyond it to study *No Longer at Ease* and *A Man of the People* which would have made interesting case studies in his context. See *The Country and the City* (London: Hogarth, 1985), 285–6.

11. Gikandi, *Reading Chinua Achebe*, 108.
12. Achebe, 'The Role of the Writer', 158.
13. Robert Holton, *Jarring Witnesses: Modern Fiction and the Representation of History* (Hemel Hempstead: Harvester Wheatsheaf, 1994).
14. Ngugi Wa Thiong'o, *Homecoming* (New York: Lawrence Hill, 1973), 54.
15. Adewale Maja-Pearce, 'Army Arrangement', *London Review of Books*, 1 April 1999, 10–13.
16. Bernth Lindfors, review of *Anthills of the Savannah* in *America*, 175:2 (20 July 1996), 23–5.

CHAPTER 5. THE TROUBLE WITH NIGERIA: *ANTHILLS OF THE SAVANNAH*

1. Eric Hobsbawm, *Age of Extremes: The Short Twentieth Century 1914–1991* (London: Michael Joseph, 1994), 3.
2. For example, 'Nigeria: Opportunities for the Private Sector' and 'Nigeria's Fourth National Development Plan', *The Times*, 16 March 1981, 11–12.
3. Ernest Gellner, *Thought and Change* (Chicago: University of Chicago Press, 1964), 169; Benedict Anderson, *Imagined Communities: Reflections on the Origin and Spread of Nationalism* (1983; rev. edn. London: Verso, 1990).
4. Ad' Obe Obe, 'The shaky national rationale', *Guardian*, 13 September 1985, 15; David Pallister,'The Plight of the Generals', *Guardian*, 13 September 1985, 13.
5. 'Biyi Bandele-Thomas, 'Wole Soyinka Interviewed 3 July 1993, Notting Hill Gate, London', in Adewale Maja-Pearce, *Wole Soyinka: An Appraisal* (Portsmouth, NH: Heinemann, 1994), 151.
6. Wole Soyinka, *The Man Died: Prison Notes of Wole Soyinka* (London: Penguin, 1975), 19, 182.
7. Elechi Amadi, *Estrangement* (London: Heinemann, 1986), 123.
8. Marjorie Winters, 'An Objective Approach to Achebe's Style', *Research in African Literatures*, 12:1 (Spring 1981), 64.
9. Ralph Ellison, Introduction to the 1982 edition of *Invisible Man* (1952), in John F. Callahan (ed.), *The Collected Essays of Ralph Ellison* (New York: Modern Library, 1995), 482.
10. See Christopher Okigbo, *Collected Poems* (London: Heinemann, 1986), 51.
11. Okigbo, 'Lament of the Silent Sisters', 57.
12. Chinua Achebe, in Anna Rutherford, 'Interview', *Kunapipi*, 9:2 (1987), 3.

13. Simon Gikandi, *Reading Chinua Achebe: Language and Ideology in Fiction* (Portsmouth, NH: Heinemann, 1991), 134.
14. C. L. Innes, *Chinua Achebe* (Cambridge: Cambridge University Press, 1990), 88.
15. For example, Carole Boyce Davies and Anne Adams Graves (eds.), *Ngambika: Studies of Women in African Literature* (Trenton, NJ: Africa World Press, 1986) and Susheila Nasta (ed.), *Motherlands: Black Women's Writing from Africa, the Caribbean and South Asia* (London: Women's Press, 1991).
16. Ato Quayson, 'Realism, Criticism, and the Disguises of Both: A Reading of Chinua Achebe's *Things Fall Apart* with an Evaluation of the Criticism Relating to It', *Research in African Literatures*, 25:4 (1994), 131.
17. See, for example, Ranu Samantrai, 'Caught at the Confluence of History: Ama Ata Aidoo's Necessary Nationalism', *Research in African Literatures*, 26:2 (1995), 140–57, and Nahem Yousaf, 'The "Public" versus the "Private" in Mariama Ba's Novels', *Journal of Commonwealth Literature*, 30:2 (1995), 85–98.
18. Innes, *Chinua Achebe*, 128.
19. Innes, *Chinua Achebe*, 133.
20. Florence Stratton, *African Literature and the Politics of Gender* (London: Routledge, 1994); Ifi Amadiume, *Male Daughters, Female Husbands: Gender and Sex in an African Society* (London: Zed, 1987).
21. See Karen J. Winkler, 'An African Writer at a Crossroads', in *The Chronicle of Higher Education*, 40:19, (12 January 1994), A12; J.O.J. Agbada Nwachukwu, 'A Conversation with Chinua Achebe', *Commonwealth Essays and Studies*, 13:1 (1990), 117–24.
22. Elleke Boehmer puts it another way, arguing that Achebe literally displaces the problem into the figurative strategies of the text itself but that in so doing he refuses to dictate women's agendas and that this is 'a significant advance' in the African novel. See 'Of Goddesses and Stories: Gender and a New Politics in Achebe's *Anthills of the Savannah*', *Kunapipi*, 12:2 (1990), 108.

CHAPTER 6. CONCLUSION: 'A BOOK BOUND IN FLESH AND BLOOD'

1. Fredric Jameson, *The Political Unconscious: Narrative as a Socially Symbolic Act* (London: Methuen, 1983), 79.
2. Chris Searle, 'Achebe and the bruised heart of Africa', *Wasafiri*, 14 (1991), 12, 16.
3. Achebe, 'Words of Anxious Love', *Guardian*, 7 May 1992, 21.

4. See, for example, Edward Said's 1993 Reith Lectures, *Representations of the Intellectual* (London: Vintage, 1994); Salman Rushdie, *Imaginary Homelands: Essays and Criticism* (London: Granta, 1991).

5. Achebe, quoted in Ezenwa-Ohaeto, *Chinua Achebe* (Oxford: James Currey, 1997), 270.

6. Anthony Smith, *The Ethnic Origins of Nations* (Oxford: Blackwell, 1986), 50.

7. Achebe, quoted in Jules Chametzky (ed.), *Black Writers Redefine Struggle: A Tribute to James Baldwin* (Amherst: University of Massachusetts Press, 1989), 74.

8. Achebe, quoted in Ezenwa-Ohaeto, *Chinua Achebe*, 257.

9. Achebe, in Amma Ogan, 'Fiction Re-orders Society', *African Guardian*, 11 February 1980.

10. James North, 'African Heart, No Darkness', *The Nation*, 10 July 2000, 39–40.

11. Ezenwa-Ohaeto, *Chinua Achebe*, 267.

12. See, for example, 'The Next Nigeria', *New Republic*, 22 March 1999, in which Achebe's response to Obasanjo's election in March of 1999 is discussed.

13. Edna Aizenberg, 'Cortazar's *Hopscotch* and Achebe's *No Longer at Ease*: Divided Heroes and Deconstructive Discourse in the Latin American and African Novel', *Okike*, February 1984, 10–26; Ezenwa-Ohaeto, *Chinua Achebe*, 260.

14. Craig Raine, 'Conrad and Prejudice', *London Review of Books*, 22 June 1989, 16–17; James North, 'African Heart'.

15. Toni Morrison, 'Home', in Wahneema Lubiano (ed.), *The House That Race Built* (New York: Vintage, 1998), 10.

16. Achebe, quoted in Ezenwa-Ohaeto, *Chinua Achebe*, 270.

17. R. N. Egudu, 'Achebe and the Igbo Narrative Tradition', *Research in African Literatures*, 12:1 (Spring 1981), 43.

18. The messages were printed in *The Weekend Concord* on 21 April 1990. Quoted in Ezenwa-Ohaeto, *Chinua Achebe*, 279.

Select Bibliography

PRIMARY MATERIAL

Fiction and non-fiction by Chinua Achebe

Things Fall Apart (1958; London: Heinemann, 1976).
No Longer at Ease (1960; London: Heinemann, 1978).
Arrow of God (1964, rev. 1974; London: Heinemann, 1986).
'The Role of the Writer in the New Nation' (a lecture delivered by Achebe to the Nigerian Library Association), *Nigeria Magazine*, 81 (1964), 157–60.
A Man of the People (1966; London: Heinemann, 1988).
Beware Soul Brother and Other Poems (London: Heinemann, 1972).
Girls at War and Other Stories (London: Heinemann, 1972).
Morning Yet on Creation Day (London: Heinemann, 1975).
The Trouble with Nigeria (London: Heinemann, 1984).
African Short Stories, co-edited with C. L. Innes (London: Heinemann, 1985).
Anthills of the Savannah (1987; London: Picador, 1988).
Hopes and Impediments (London: Heinemann, 1988).
The South Bank lecture of 1990, published as 'African Literature as Restoration of Celebration', in Kirsten Holst Petersen and Anna Rutherford, *Chinua Achebe: A Celebration* (Portsmouth, NH: Heinemann, 1991), 1–10.
The Heinemann Book of Contemporary African Stories, co-edited with C. L. Innes (Oxford: Heinemann, 1992).
Home and Exile (Oxford: Oxford University Press, 2000).

Monographs and edited books about Achebe

Carroll, David, *Chinua Achebe* (London: Macmillan, 1990). Carroll's introduction to Achebe and his work takes as its starting point the consensus view that Achebe contests European representations of Africans by basing his fictions solidly in Igbo cosmology.

Ezenwa-Ohaeto, *Chinua Achebe: A Biography* (Oxford: James Currey, 1997). This former student of Achebe's has produced a straightforward and clearly written biography that reveals few if any surprises. Especially good on Achebe's formative years.

Gikandi, Simon, *Reading Chinua Achebe: Language and Ideology in Fiction* (Portsmouth, NH: Heinemann, 1991). A wide-ranging and theoretically informed reading of Achebe's novels.

Innes, C. L., *Chinua Achebe* (Cambridge University Press, 1990). A more ambitious study than Carroll's, Innes provides a Bakhtinian reading of Achebe's fiction in order to argue that he has 'Africanized' the novel form.

Innes, C. L., and Berth Lindfors (eds.), *Critical Perspectives on Chinua Achebe* (London: Heinemann, 1979). A collection of essays that includes contributions from Abiola Irele, Ngugi wa Thiong'o, David Carroll and Gareth Griffiths.

Iyasere, Solomon O., *Understanding Things Fall Apart: Selected Essays and Criticism* (New York: The Whitson Publishing Company, 1998). A selection of previously published essays examining various thematic and stylistic aspects of *Things Fall Apart*.

Killam, G. D., *The Writings of Chinua Achebe* (London: Heinemann, 1969).

Moore, Gerald, *Seven African Writers* (London: Oxford University Press, 1962). Includes an early critical response to Achebe's *Things Fall Apart* and *No Longer at Ease*, entitled 'Chinua Achebe: Nostalgia and Realism'.

Njoku, Benedict Chiaka, *Four Novels of Chinua Achebe* (New York: Peter Lang, 1984).

Ojinmah, Umelo, *Chinua Achebe: New Perspectives* (Ibadan, Nigeria: Spectrum Books, 1991).

Omotoso, Kole, *Achebe or Soyinka? A Study in Contrasts* (London: Hans Zell, 1996). An excellent idea to compare Nigeria's two most acclaimed writers but this is an uneven study which includes a few mistakes of fact. It is premised on and concludes with the idea that Achebe and Soyinka are caught in ethnic cul-de-sacs: Achebe boxed into the Igbo and Soyinka the Yoruba tradition.

Petersen, Kirsten Holst, and Anna Rutherford, *Chinua Achebe: A Celebration* (Portsmouth, NH: Heinemann, 1991). A collection of essays celebrating Achebe's life. This collection also contains a very informative discussion of Achebe's role as Commissioning Editor for Heinemann's African Writers Series.

Ravenscroft, Arthur, *Chinua Achebe* (Harlow: Longmans, Green and Co. Ltd, 1969). An early study that provides some biographical context and useful summaries of Achebe's novels from *Things Fall Apart* to *A Man of the People*. A study that is very much of its time.

Articles

An enormous number of articles have been written about Achebe and his work. The following list is not intended to be comprehensive but provides examples of recent criticism that should be widely available.

Aizenberg, Edna, 'Cortazar's *Hopscotch* and Achebe's *No Longer at Ease*: Divided Heroes and Deconstructive Discourse in the Latin American and African Novel', *Okike* (February 1984), 10–26.

Boehmer, Elleke, 'Of Goddesses and Stories: Gender and a New Politics in Achebe's *Anthills of the Savannah*', *Kunapipi*, 12:2 (1990), 102–13.

Brown, Hugh R., 'Igbo Words for the Non-Igbo: Achebe's Artistry in *Arrow of God*', *Research in African Literatures*, 12:1 (1981), 69–85.

Egudu, R. N., 'Achebe and the Igbo Narrative Tradition', *Research in African Literatures*, 12:1 (Spring 1981), 43–54. Egudu reads a series of anecdotes and discusses the ways in which they are used as illustration and dramatization or employed for mitigating the intensity of a situation. He argues that Achebe's greatest contribution is the effective translation of an Igbo art form into the African novel.

Griffiths, Gareth, 'Chinua Achebe: When Did You Last See Your Father?', *World Literature Written in English*, 27:1 (1987), 18–27. Griffiths asserts that there is a novel 'missing' between *Things Fall Apart* and *No Longer at Ease* because Achebe's own father died young and his biographical sense of the kinds of issues that might concern his character Nwoye/Isaac was therefore curtailed.

JanMohamed, Abdul, 'Sophisticated Primitivism: The Syncretism of Oral and Literate Modes in Achebe's *Things Fall Apart*', *Ariel*, 15:4 (1984), 19–39. An example of the important cultural work that this postcolonial critic began in *Manichean Aesthetics* in reading Achebe within an informed critical context.

Ikegami, Robin, 'Knowledge and Power, The Story and the Storyteller: Achebe's *Anthills of the Savannah*', *Modern Fiction Studies*, 37:3 (1991), 493–507.

Kortenaar, Neil Ten, 'How the Centre is Made to Hold in *Things Fall Apart*', *English Studies in Canada*, 17:3 (1991), 319–36. Kortenaar deploys Claude Levi-Strauss and Michel Foucault to suggest that 'the West's knowledge of the world is as culture-based and time-bound as any other knowledge'. He then applies his findings to Achebe's notions of epistemology as explored in *Things Fall Apart*.

—‛ "Only connect": *Anthills of the Savannah* and Achebe's *Trouble with Nigeria*', *Research in African Literatures*, 24:3 (1993), 59–72.

MacDougall, Russell, 'Achebe's *Arrow of God*: The Kinetic Idiom of Unmasking', *Kunapipi*, 9:2 (1987), 8–24.

—'The "Problem of Locomotion" in *No Longer At Ease*', *World Literature Written in English*, 29:1 (1989), 19–25. This essay provides a close reading of the novel by focusing on organizational metaphors – walking, driving, travelling, dancing – and their relationship with Igbo aesthetics and Western values.

North, James, 'African Heart, No Darkness', *The Nation*, 10 July 2000, 39–41. While reviewing Achebe's *Home and Exile*, North explores why he thinks V. S. Naipaul has received more attention in the West than Achebe.

Obiechina, Emmanuel, 'Narrative Proverbs in the African Novel', *Research in African Literatures*, 24:4 (1993), 123–40. This essay details the ways in which Achebe's embedded stories in *Things Fall Apart* (fables, tales, proverbs) provide a detailed commentary on the action.

Quayson, Ato, 'Realism, Criticism, and the Disguises of Both: A Reading of Chinua Achebe's *Things Fall Apart* with an Evaluation of the Criticism Relating to It', *Research in African Literatures*, 25:4 (1994), 129–36. Quayson's essay challenges some of the earlier criticism of *Things Fall Apart*, particularly that which sought to read the Nigerian novel as a realist text. For Quayson realism, and the uses to which it is put, remains problematic in its reliance on mimeticism.

Rogers, Philip, '*No Longer at Ease*: Chinua Achebe's "Heart of Whiteness" ', *Research in African Literatures*, 14:2 (1983), 165–83.

Smith, Angela, 'The Mouth With Which to Tell of Their Suffering: The Role of the Narrator and Reader in Achebe's *Things Fall Apart*', *Commonwealth Essays and Studies*, 7:1 (1988), 77–90.

Swann, Joseph, 'From *Things Fall Apart* to *Anthills of the Savannah*: The Changing Face of History in Chinua Achebe's Novels', in G. V. Davies and H. Maes-Jelinek (eds.), *Crisis and Creativity in the New Literatures in English* (Amsterdam: Rodopi, 1991), 191–202.

Udumukwu, Onyemaechi, 'Achebe and the Negation of Independence', *Modern Fiction Studies*, 37:3 (1991), 471–91.

Watts, Cedric, ' "A Bloody Racist": About Achebe's Views on Conrad', *Yearbook of English Studies* (1983), 196–209. A classic article in which Watts engages with Achebe's criticism of Conrad and judges that anger clouds the Nigerian writer's judgement. Of a series of articles that follow a similar line, this is one of the most balanced.

Winkler, Karen J., 'An African Writer at a Crossroads', in *The Chronicle of Higher Education*, 40:19 (12 January 1994), A9, A12. Although brief, this is a careful overview of Achebe's ideas about fiction-writing as they arise out of an interview with the author.

Winters, Marjorie, 'An Objective Approach to Achebe's Style', *Research in African Literatures*, 12:1 (Spring 1981), 55–68. Winters employs a stylistic approach to study the novels quantitatively by sampling sections and studying syntactical structures. There are difficulties with such a formalist study (she suggests her 'objective' approach should be deployed by non-African critics of African literature) but some interesting points are raised.

Interviews

'Chinua Achebe', in *African Writers Talking*, ed. Dennis Duerden and Cosmo Pieterse (New York: Africana Publishing Co., 1972), 3–17. This is a series of short interviews with Achebe, conducted between 1962 and 1967 by three different interviewers.

Botstein, Leon, 'Things Fall Together: A Conversation with Chinua Achebe and Toni Morrison', *Transition: An International Review*, 11:1 (2001), 150–65. This article is a summary of the public conversation that took place between the two authors in 2000.

Currey, James, Alan Hill and Keith Sambrook in conversation with Kirsten Holst Petersen, 'Working with Chinua Achebe: The African Writers Series', in Kirsten Holst Petersen and Anna Rutherford, *Chinua Achebe: A Celebration* (Portsmouth, NH: Heinemann, 1991), 149–59.

Nwachukwu-Agbada, J. O. J., 'A Conversation with Chinua Achebe', *Commonwealth Essays and Studies*, 13:1 (1990), 117–24. This interview was conducted shortly before the publication of *Anthills of the Savannah*. It includes some interesting responses to questions about critical coteries that believe all writing should be ideologically committed and to questions about the novel form.

Ogbaa, Kalu, 'An Interview with C A', *Research in African Literatures*, 12:1 (Spring 1981), 1–13. Achebe reiterates that in his view European culture disturbed rather than destroyed Igbo culture and exemplifies the ways in which this is conveyed in the early novels. He goes on to discuss critical responses to his work.

Rowell, C. H., 'An Interview with Chinua Achebe', *Callaloo*, 13:1 (1990), 86–101.

Rutherford, Anna, 'Interview', *Kunapipi*, 9:2 (1987), 1–7. Rutherford asks specifically about *Anthills of the Savannah* in what is a brief but interesting interview.

Searle, Chris, 'Achebe and the Bruised Heart of Africa', *Wasafiri*, 14 (1991), 12–16.

Wilkinson, Jane (ed.), *Talking with African Writers* (London: James Currey, 1990). Includes an interview with Achebe, pp. 46–57.

Useful websites

There are a number of websites that readers may wish to visit. Some of these have links to other relevant sites. I have not attempted to distinguish the main focus of each site, as many contain a variety of information. For example, biographical information, reviews, interviews, etc.

http://www.scholars.nus.edu.sg/landow/post/achebeov.html
http://www.wsu.edu:80007brians/anglophone/achebe.html
http://www.litincontext.com/things/timeline4.html
http://www.bbc.co.uk/history/programmes/centurions/achebe/achbiog.shtml
http://www.sdsmt.edu/courses/is/hum375/africa.html
http://www.usafricaonline.com/chidoachebe.html
http://www.conjunctions.com/archives/c17-ca.html
http://www.usaafricaonline.com/achebe70.html

SECONDARY MATERIAL

The following is just a small sample of relevant material. Readers are encouraged to consult the bibliographies contained in these texts.

Booth, James, *Writers and Politics in Nigeria* (London: Hodder and Stoughton, 1981). A general overview of the nation and its politics and the ways in which a range of writers begin to respond in stories and novels.

Ahmad, Aijaz, *In Theory* (London: Verso, 1992).

Amuta, Chidi, *The Theory of African Literature* (London: Zed Books, 1989).

Ashcroft, Bill, et al., *The Empire Writes Back* (London: Routledge, 1989).

——*The Post-Colonial Reader* (London: Routledge, 1995).

Azim, Firdous, *The Colonial Rise of the Novel* (London: Routledge, 1993).

Bhabha, Homi, *The Location of Culture* (London: Routledge, 1994).

Boehmer, Elleke, *Empire Writing: An Anthology of Colonial Literature, 1870–1918* (Oxford: Oxford University Press, 1999).

——*Colonial and Postcolonial Literature* (Oxford: Oxford University Press, 1995).

Bristow, Joseph, *Empire Boys: Adventures in a Man's World* (London: HarperCollins, 1991).

Chinweizu, et al., *Toward the Decolonisation of African Literature* (London: KPI Limited, 1985).

Davies, Carole Boyce, and A. A. Graves (eds.), *Ngambika: Studies of Women in African Literature* (Trenton, NJ: Africa World Press, 1986).

Fanon, Frantz, *Black Skin, White Masks* (London: Pluto, 1986).

——*The Wretched of the Earth* (London: Penguin, 1990).

Giddings, Robert (ed.), *Literature and Imperialism* (London: Macmillan, 1991).

Gugelberger, Georg (ed.), *Marxism and African Literature* (Trenton, NJ: Africa World Press, 1986).

Harlow, Barbara, *Resistance Literature* (London: Methuen, 1987).

JanMohamed, Abdul, 'The Economy of Manichean Allegory: The Function of Racial Difference in Colonialist Literature', *Critical Inquiry*, 12 (Autumn 1985), 59–87.

——*Manichean Aesthetics: The Politics of Literature in Colonial Africa* (Amherst: University of Massachusetts Press, 1983).

Maier, Karl, *This House Has Fallen: Nigeria in Crisis* (London: Penguin, 2000 or 2001). Maier reels off the kinds of statistics that make the reader's head spin – figures for national debt, oil revenue, national illiteracy, kleptocracy – in his incisive overview of what has happened to Nigeria since Independence. He includes statements from former unrepentant heads of state and concludes that the country has been bled dry economically.

Maja-Pearce, Adewale, *In My Father's Country: A Nigerian Journey* (London: Heinemann, 1987). An autobiographical journey by a writer whose father is Nigerian and whose mother is English that plays off the author's insider–outsider status.

Moore-Gilbert, Bart, *Postcolonial Theory: Contexts, Practices, Politics* (London: Verso, 1997).

Nasta, Susheila (ed.), *Motherlands: Black Women's Writing from Africa, the Caribbean and South Asia* (London: The Women's Press, 1991).

Ngugi wa Thiong'o, *Writers in Politics* (London: Heinemann, 1981).

——*Decolonising the Mind: The Politics of Language in African Literature* (London: James Currey, 1986).

Obiechina, Emmanuel, *An African Popular Literature* (Cambridge: Cambridge University Press, 1973).

Parry, Benita, *Conrad and Imperialism: Ideological Boundaries and Visionary Frontiers* (London: Macmillan, 1983).
——'Problems in Current Theories of Colonial Discourse', *The Oxford Literary Review*, 5:1–2 (1987), 27–58.
Rushdie, Salman, *Imaginary Homelands* (London: Granta 1991).
Said, Edward, *Culture and Imperialism* (London: Chatto and Windus, 1993).
——*Orientalism* (1978; London: Penguin, 1991).
Schipper, Mineke, *Beyond the Boundaries: African Literature and Literary Theory* (London: Allison and Busby, 1989).
Soyinka, Wole, *The Burden of Memory: The Muse of Forgiveness* (Oxford University Press, 1999). An example of Soyinka going through the painful process of national critique within the specific socio-cultural context of cultural memory.
——*Myth, Literature and the African World* (Cambridge: Cambridge University Press, 1978).
——*The Open Sore of a Continent: A Personal Narrative of the Nigerian Crisis* (Oxford: Oxford University Press, 1996). This is a sensitive study of nations, states and the predicament of postcolonial fall-out in which the former Nigerian poet laureate who was detained, charged with high treason and exiled takes an intellectual turn around his former homeland ('I accept Nigeria as a responsibility').
Spivak, Gayatri, *In Other Worlds* (London: Routledge, 1987).
Stratton, Florence, *Contemporary African Literature and the Politics of Gender* (London: Routledge, 1994).
Williams, Patrick, and Laura Chrisman, *Colonial Discourse and Postcolonial Theory* (Hemel Hempstead: Harvester Wheatsheaf, 1994).
Young, Robert, *Colonial Desire: Hybridity in Theory, Culture and Race* (London: Routledge, 1995).
——*White Mythologies: Writing History and the West* (London: Routledge, 1990).

Index